Making the Right Connections:
A Guide for Nature Writers

By James Heintzman

Michael Gross and Ronald Zimmerman, Editors

Illustrated by Sylvia Myrhe

UW-SP FOUNDATION PRESS, INC.
UNIVERSITY OF WISCONSIN
STEVENS POINT
STEVENS POINT, WI 54481

Making the Right Connections:
A Guide for Nature Writers

ISBN 0-932310-07-9

Library of Congress Catalog Card Number 87-051662

About the Interpreter's Handbook Series

A Guide for Nature Writers is the first in a series of practical guides written for interpretive professionals and students.

For more information, contact:

Dr. Michael Gross
College of Natural Resources
University of Wisconsin-Stevens Point
Stevens Point, WI 54481

These guides have been developed with the support of:

University of Wisconsin - Stevens Point Foundation
University of Wisconsin - Stevens Point College of Natural Resources
Association of Interpretive Naturalists - Region 5

CONTENTS

Acknowledgements

Books, like ideas, are joint efforts. Everything you read or hear has some influence upon your writing and thinking. I would like to thank all of the writers who have shown me the magic of words making the right connections.

I want to thank the people who made this book about writing and thinking a reality. Dr. Michael Gross and Ronald Zimmerman have been involved from the beginning to end, from suggesting the book to its publication. Dr. Don Pattow and Dr. Lowell Klessig also gave generously of their time and expertise, reviewing the manuscript and suggesting needed improvements. Char Pingel skillfully guided the manuscript electronically to its final format.

My wife, Joan, read and edited a multitude of drafts, provided solutions and typed the completed manuscript. She also gave me the support and encouragement I needed for the long, involved process of putting my ideas into print.

This book is better because of these efforts, but responsibility for any errors or shortcomings is cheerfully accepted by the author.

Dedication

To Joan - of course.

PREFACE

Don't worry about what you are writing; worry about what they are reading.   — Anonymous

That is good advice for any writer to remember; for the interpretive writer, it is essential. Writing has no meaning unless it is read; it has no impact unless it touches the reader. The connection between reader and writer is the essence of interpretive writing.

Just putting words down on paper is difficult for most of us. When we also face deadlines and public scrutiny, it can seem overwhelming. As a county naturalist, one of my many duties was writing a weekly nature column for a local newspaper. I enjoyed writing it and people continually told me they enjoyed reading it. People meeting me for the first time greeted me like an old friend and told me which columns they especially appreciated. Teachers clipped out columns for bulletin boards and parents sent copies to their grown children in other states. Some people even took the time to write approving letters to the editor. Somehow I made connections with a great many different people through my column.

I have since studied the art and science of writing in more detail, trying to find the elements that go into the connections between writers and readers. This guide is a distillation of my findings and feelings on the subject. It offers no secret formulas for becoming a famous nature writer; it is simply a guide for anyone who wants to write nature columns and articles that are read by other people.

If it helps you become a better writer, it will be because you remember the opening quotation and take it to heart.

1

I WISH I HAD SAID THAT!
Sources of Information and Inspiration

To see a world in a grain of sand
And a heaven in a wild flower
Hold infinity in the palm of your hand
And eternity in an hour.

— William Blake

Finding a fresh topic or a new approach is a never ending challenge for any writer. A nature writer, however, has a special advantage; there is a constant parade of fascinating material passing by just outside the door.

Share Real Experiences

Sharing personal experiences makes your writing more lively and exciting because real adventures are always more interesting than recycled facts. If you are ever at a loss for words when you look at a blank sheet of paper, get up and go outside where things are happening. If you cannot find an interesting topic, you are not really looking. If you are trying to explain the effects of seasonal temperature variations on physiological phenomena in trees, go to a sugarbush on a frosty March morning and help make some maple syrup. If you are going to write about marsh ecology, go out and get your feet wet. If you want to discuss bird flight, watch barn swallows demonstrate the principles involved. Real events are always more fun than abstract concepts. That is why you want to write about them.

Keep A Journal

Memories are never as clear or complete as we would like them to be. Even vivid events fade away more quickly than we realize; that is why a written record of your experiences is essential to your success in writing. Keeping a daily journal will do more than just provide you with fresh, accurate and on-the-spot descriptions; it will also make you more aware of recurring changes and make you a better observer. If you note such phenomena as spring flowers blooming in schoolhouse windows and in the woods, you will realize that nature's cycles are a subject of deep common interest.

Any small notebook will serve for field notes and quick sketches, but you may prefer a hard-cover sketchbook or blank ledger book for a daily journal. Careful observations and detailed notes in any form are important sources of information for a writer. Even if reference books and other materials are accurate, they may not be pertinent to your particular area or situation. In any case, their information will be incomplete and second-hand.

Know What You Are Seeing

Any experience is made richer by understanding. The more you know about a subject, the more you can appreciate all of its qualities. You should research your subject as thoroughly as possible before you begin to write about it.

Scientific societies publish newsletters and other materials that highlight current findings in particular disciplines. Both popular magazines and standard reference books provide general information that can be supplemented by further research. You should also have a list of experts that can be contacted personally if you cannot find the answers to particular questions.

If you merely repeat in different words what you have read elsewhere, however, you omit an important element of interpretive writing. You are just passing on information.

Write About Your Interests

Your enthusiasm for a subject will shine through your writing, but if you show no interest, neither will your readers. Since every subject has the potential to be fascinating, it is up to you to discover what interesting aspects a subject has to offer. Even if you lack feeling and understanding for a subject, you can still share someone else's interest.

The Familiar and the Bizarre

One easy way to capture a reader's attention is to reveal new and surprising facts about familiar, everyday things. Every natural object has a fascinating story to tell; all it takes to uncover it is a little time and effort.

Try to imagine how the world would be changed if a particular subject suddenly disappeared. What if there were no more bees or beetles? What would the world be like if flowers had never evolved? Questions like these do not have simple answers, but they can make you more appreciative of common objects. Surprisingly, things we take most for granted are often the most important. Try to imagine a world without dust, for example. How do those tiny airborne particles affect the way the earth works?

If you write about animals that reproduce without sex or plants that eat animals, you are sure to stimulate interest. Sex and violence are perennially popular subjects and they will undoubtedly continue to be popular as long as people communicate. Such subjects demand careful handling, of course; it is just as easy to offend readers as it is to attract their attention.

The things we fear and loathe also hold us spellbound. A snake held up for observation may cause people to express shock and disgust, but they usually watch the snake intently from the edge of the crowd gathered around it. We may feel sympathy for small creatures preyed upon by larger, more powerful animals, but we still would rather watch an owl instead of a mouse.

Mysterious creatures that live in unfamiliar worlds and show strange behavior and unusual adaptations fascinate us because they are unknown. Since we actually know very little about any creature, there is no end of fascinating subjects to write about. Just look for the mysterious and unusual in every subject you deal with.

Listen to Real People

If you spend all of your time with biologists and birds you will certainly become more knowledgeable, but you may have trouble relating that knowledge to other people. Those who already share your appreciation do not need more convincing; write for the people who do not care.

If you want to reach a wider audience, you must get out and talk with them. Find out what people are talking about and you may realize what they are likely to read. Reading popular magazines or watching television may not always be inspiring, but it can be illuminating. When viewed with a critical eye, commercials and advertisements can give you new insights into popular tastes and attitudes. After all, billions of dollars are spent every year to understand and influence public opinion. You may as well take advantage of such efforts. Merely copying mass marketing techniques, of course, means appealing to the lowest common denominator, and your readers are already assailed too often by such manipulative methods. Insincerity can be easily spotted by discerning readers.

Remember the Reader

The human element should always be part of your topic, either directly or indirectly. Natural history topics may be fascinating in themselves, but people relate best with other people. Since even naturalists have a tendency to separate humans from the natural scheme of things, remind yourself continually that people are part of your subject. You can incorporate people into your writing by talking about historical figures associated with your subject. A discussion of tomatoes, for instance, might mention Christopher Columbus and Thomas Jefferson, at least in passing. Even an anonymous historical character has more in common with your readers than any non-human subject. Use real people to relate your story to the reader. How did pioneers look at or use your subject? Which scientists first studied its secrets? How does it affect people today? What does your neighbor think?

Answer Questions

Specialists seldom realize that other people do not share their particular expertise and knowledge. Even the most basic workings and features of the natural environment may be mysteries to the uninitiated; do not assume that everyone is as familiar with them as you are. On the other hand, you should be careful not to talk down to the reader. This balance is difficult to maintain, but it helps to remember the old observation that writers usually overestimate their readers' knowledge and underestimate their intelligence.

If anybody is reading your column, they will soon be asking you questions about a wide variety of topics. This is your opportunity to find out what people do and do not know—and what they would like to know. If you listen to them carefully and anticipate future questions, your writing will be more relevant and up to date.

Besides That...

Topics for columns are limited only by your imagination and interests. If none of the preceding suggestions seem to fit a particular situation, you can always fall back on some standard formats.

For example, you can lead your readers on a walk that you have recently taken. Although excursions can be quiet and relatively uneventful, you might also consider a canoe trip, a wildlife research operation, a search for a rare fern or flower, or an outdoor adventure with a lively group of children. When you do interesting things, it is much easier to find interesting subjects to write about.

Even if your job is keeping you indoors, you can still do a personal profile of a particular plant or animal. (This would be a "Meet the Red Fox" style of article, an ever-ready standby.)

You can always take any common item and trace it back to its beginnings in the natural world. Consider the paper clip, for example. What steps are involved? How were people involved along the way? Where did it start? Where does it go? Why?

You can use special topics like nature's misunderstood villains or the antics of individual animals. Natural engineering and design, scientific quests, life we cannot see, or the life we pass by unseeing are other basic topics.

The study of word origins, or etymology, has some surprising revelations to make as well. Common names and folk names often carry an amazing amount of history. Scientific nomenclature is not always as straightforward and objective as it appears on the surface. A little research in a good dictionary or book of word origins will show you that words are much more than simple identification tags. For example, the word "human" comes from an ancient root meaning "earth" and the world "world" comes from the root meaning "man." The word "learning" comes from an old word meaning "to track or trail." Connections like these give a unity to both learning and language and provide a wealth of interesting speculations. Who named the "daisy" or "day's eye?" Is lungwort really useful for treating colds? Where did the junco get its name?

If you still have a problem finding a topic, you can always write about environmental problems. It is best to remember, though, that most people have enough to worry about. If you have to add another to their list, be sure to show how the problem affects them directly and be sure to tell them what they can do about it.

Basic concepts of biology or other sciences can be entertaining and informative if you provide illustrations and example from everyday life. What unique properties of water make ice fishing possible? What does plant succession have to do with how your readers spend their weekends? What can water running down a drain tell your readers about weather patterns? Remember, most people do not like to be lectured to.

How-to-do-it columns are sometimes difficult to pull off. Explaining even the basics of a project or activity often requires a surprising amount of words and illustrations. The best you should hope for is a kindling of interest in the reader. Be sure to include sources of further information. This type of column is perhaps most useful as a promotion for an upcoming demonstration program.

A Few More Suggestions...

Write about a personal discovery.

Write about something you know nothing about.

Write about something you think you know all about.

Write about something that happens only at this time of the year.

Show how things are designed to do a job.

Write about something everyone is experiencing.

Show how a common object is unique (backyard wonders).

Show hidden connections.

Show what a thing does instead of what it is.

Go back into the past or forward into the future.

Remember that the more you learn and experience, the more you will have to offer.

or...?

A WRITING SAMPLER

Cold and bright and thirty-one days long, March holds the turning of the year in the folds of its weeks and, most often, buffets us with winter more than it laves us in spring.

Nature manages all the year long, to appear undependable, capricious, whimsical, even mad; but never quite so outrageously so as this third wild month when the violet blossoming on the sunny bank is likely to have its blue eye filled with snow, and the groundhog, nibbling sweet new clover in the lee of gray stones will most surely be driven back into his burrow by raw and biting winds.

March winds have to blow, I'm told. It is one of the few things you can depend upon about March. Masses of cold air have accumulated in the arctic regions while the sun has been off in the south, increasing the heat of the shimmering tropics. Strong currents, now, are flowing south from the cold regions, and other currents equally strong are flowing north from the warm ones, and when the two systems collide, or play leapfrog, the proverbial winds of March result.

Wild winds they are, and mad winds, but they help to dry the earth left oozing and soggy from winter; they play a tremendous part in the vital turning-over of the waters in lakes and ponds, and they stimulate the circulation of life juices in trees and lesser plants.

Those trees and lesser plants know another dependable thing about March: its sunlight. Not that today will be sunny - or that it won't - but that the sun is there above the horizon, just a little longer on each successive day. The sun and its heat and light are irresistible. The snow has to go, the ice has to melt, the earth has to warm, eggs have to hatch and roots have to stretch and grow.

Each life was shut down for the winter with its own special code for awakening in the spring, and the key that triggers the opening mechanism is the sun's light and warmth. Insects, both eggs and over-wintering adults, are quickly warmed, and so are the surface rootings of quick-growing plants; but it takes a little longer for warmth to reach the turtle, the earthworm, and the frog.

And that is another amazing thing about chaotic March—its ultimate orderliness. Whether spring comes in on a long, slow curve, or whether it arrives with a warm wind and a hot sun all in one week, everything happens in its own time. Nothing gets out of its place in line.

The robin does not arrive in any numbers before the earthworms unthread themselves from the tangles in their dark cellars. The first butterflies that drift about the woodlands drink tree sap and are not dependent upon the nectar of flowers yet to bloom. And many a flying insect is livening up the marshes before the first frogs arise from the mud.

It is the old food chain again, and the first to arrive is he who gets eaten—the tiniest, the least able to fight back. And that is why I begin, sometime during the first week of March, to bring back from each morning's walk a dropper of water taken from the warming shallows of the pond or from a sunny puddle in the marsh. Under the lens of a microscope, in the amazing world of the water drop, on a certain morning I shall see some unbelievable creature moving about. He will be seeking, of course, his own tinier food and at the same time inadvertently offering himself upon the table of the next higher order—some tiny crustacean, or the larval form of an insect.

I am never quite sure that the first animalcule I find was not warmed out of his encystment in my pocket or, for that matter, on the glass slide itself; but if, in the next day or so, his numbers and kinds increase then I can say to myself, "Well, spring is here." But I say it under my breath, for there is tremendous discontinuity between the world of winter-bound humanity and the one under the lens. However, now I can walk through the wet places knowing that the life I sense with all my being is truly stirring there.

Then comes a day when I find small flies and tiny gnats busy about the fleshy flowerheads in the twisted spathes of skunk cabbage, and the catkins hanging loose and free on the alder bushes by the stream. I nod my head. "Spring is here." But still I say it softly.

And one morning, in a sunny curve of the stream bank where the water flows quietly, I shall find half a dozen water striders standing about on the surface of the water, looking dazed and newly arrived and not knowing what to do about it. Every now and then two or three will drift together, then solemnly disentangle their long legs and stand about as before. And I shall make up for their apparent lack of joyousness by smiling broadly, for I love water striders (and privately call them minnie skippers), and I shall say aloud but still to myself, "Well, spring is really here."

And then comes an afternoon when the sun lies warm and bright like a golden veil across the meadow and the marshes. A tiny sleigh bell tinkles. Another sleigh bell rings. And suddenly, the once-winter world is filled with the wildly tintinabulating chorus of the spring peepers as they gather for their primeval rites, and I say joyously, and aloud, and to everyone I meet, "Spring is here! The peepers are back!" And everyone with half an ear responds, "I know!"

"The Search for Spring"
in Wildlings, by Mary Leister

Unraveling the Threads:

How do you like this selection? What particular things did you like or dislike? Do you think it is well-written? Why or why not? How does it illustrate or contradict the points made in the last chapter? This is a column that first appeared in the Baltimore Sun. You may wish to read the rest of the columns selected for her book.

Mary Leister's writing shows her talent as an active and accurate observer. Her subjects may be familiar, but her treatments never are. Study her writing skills with an eye to her methods of leading the reader through her experiences. Organization is the subject of the next chapter and her writing offers a good example.

After an intriguing opening statement of her subject she moves on quickly to illustrate with real examples. Her personality comes through her writing style and her choice of images, but it does not intrude upon what she is describing. Note the active images and use of contrast.

Note how wind, as a symbol of change, is used as a transition between the second and third paragraphs. The contrasting elements of dependability and uncertainty are incorporated into her explanation of the reason for winds and the whimsical nature of March, things that the readers are experiencing first-hand.

Winds also serve as a transition to the next paragraph, but now they are shown to be more than a nuisance. The idea of circulating winds leads naturally into water, something readers can depend upon seeing in March. She then ties in melting water, rising temperatures and stretching tree roots into the subject of her next paragraph—increased light and warmth.

The effects are shown as steady and dependable, in contrast to the wild stirrings described in the previous paragraph. Three examples—the turtle, the earthworm, and the frog—are still waiting quietly in the earth beneath stretching tree roots.

The idea of an intricate order behind the apparent chaos suggested in the last paragraph is developed and then summarized in one clear statement: "Nothing gets out of its place in line."

Again, three illustrations are given, this time involving creatures of the air. A connection to the earth images used before is made with the first example, an earthworm and a robin. Note that in this paragraph, the illustrations are all paired relationships—the subject of the next paragraph.

She gives the reason for the order described and shifts smoothly into a description of her search for the smallest and earliest sign of active life in the melted waters of March.

Her doubts about these almost invisible signs of spring again bring up feelings of uncertainty. Her doubt also mirrors the probable opinion of her readers on the matter. Nevertheless, she writes a quoted statement of certainty—with reservations.

She then proceeds to a description of larger stirrings, including plants. Another stage of progression is accompanied by another quoted statement of certainty (in slightly different form), but there is still lingering doubt—and rising tension.

Life moves at a faster pace in the next paragraph. The examples are again described in vivid and personal terms. Again there is a tentative statement of certainty, slightly rephrased. This builds the tensions and draws the reader into the final paragraph.

The tension built up through the entire article is finally released with a description of the real sign of spring. Note how the phrase "cold and bright" in the first paragraph is now "warm and bright."

Any lingering uncertainty of spring's arrival is dispelled by a ringing chorus, an unequivocal statement of the fact, and a final collective "I know!"

The organization of this piece is an inherent part of its message.

2

ONE OF THESE DAYS I HAVE TO GET ORGANIZED...
Pulling Everything Together

All things near and far
Hiddenly to each other
Linked are
That thou canst not pluck a flower
Without troubling a star.

—Francis Thompson

Do it now!

Regardless of how we feel about it, organization is essential for good writing. It is not an extra, it is not something we do if there is enough time. Putting down ideas and words in a meaningful order **is** writing. Taking time at the beginning to organize information not only makes writing better, it makes it easier, too. Any time spent preparing ideas is amply repaid later. Besides making the job of writing simpler, good organization also makes writing easier to follow. And making things easier for your readers is also essential for good writing.

Getting Started

Before you put any words on paper, you should ask yourself some questions:

Who am I trying to reach?

Who am I talking to?

What do I want them to hear?

What do I want them to remember?

Once you have a clearer picture of your readers and the purpose of your column, you can start collecting the information you need to write it. Collect facts and images from as many sources as

possible; even if you do not use all of them, they will add to your understanding of the subject. Seeking new information is a vital step; it is when we think we know something that we stop wondering and learning about it.

Your background information should include some basic facts: common characteristics and habits, seasonal changes, interrelationships, other people's findings and experiences, and unique qualities. Do not judge the merit or importance of facts at this stage of the process. Write down items that catch your attention and fancy. Look for details that explain, instruct, entertain, and amaze. The ability to scan large amounts of material quickly is a valuable skill for writers under the pressure of deadlines. Like other skills, it improves with practice. It is a good practice to write down ideas and information in your own words, right from the start, unless you will be quoting directly. This will help you avoid a disjointed writing style.

The facts you put down may not tell the whole story, but they can make it more real for the reader. Interesting facts that can be stored away in the back of the mind or shared with someone else gives your writing relevance and legitimacy. If a reader can say "That's interesting!" or "I didn't know that!" he will feel that the time and effort spent reading has been rewarded. People enjoy acquiring and trading information as well as money.

Where to Look

If you do not already have a good-sized personal reference library, it is time to get started. Public libraries cannot be expected to have on hand all of the books you need or the materials you want. You should also keep an on-going file of newspaper and magazine clippings, notes, and feature articles from whatever sources you find in your daily reading. Reading widely not only adds to your store of knowledge, it makes you more aware of both good and bad writing. Note how different writers present similar subjects in different types of magazines and books. See how each magazine's editorial style is reflected in each of its different articles. What makes good writing enjoyable to read? What makes bad writing noticeable almost immediately?

Get It Down On Paper

If you want to remember something, write it down right away, and be sure it does not get lost in the shuffle. Standard index cards can be carried anywhere for quick note-taking, but they have a tendency to get mixed up or lost entirely. Inexpensive writing tablets, bound notebooks, and legal pads work well for putting down facts and writing first drafts. Even a single sheet of paper can easily hold more facts than you can work into a single column, but the unused facts do not have to go to waste. After you are done, each sheet of information on a subject can go into the appropriate section of your personal reference file. Any subject has enough information to make up a multitude of columns.

Next...Take a Break

Once you have collected all of the pertinent facts and recorded them, you should simply walk away and leave them alone for awhile. Do not rearrange the order of just a few items or play around with a phrase or two. Set everything aside and do something else - even if it is only for a short time.

Your mind will not be able to leave it alone, anyway. This is the time to let images and ideas drift freely in your subconscious or in the metaphoric part of your brain. If you immediately try to arrange everything in an orderly manner, there is little room left for creativity. Even a short break allows you to come back with a fresh, clear view of the subject. Do not consider this break as mere procrastination; it is an important step in the writing process.

Organize!

Your goal in organizing your material should be distinct ideas arranged in logical sequences. Methods of organization may vary, but the ultimate result should be a smooth, effortless flow of thought. You can always use chronological order, go from generalities to specifics, or use other standard arrangements, but they may not always fit your needs. There is no one correct way to organize your thoughts or information; you have to decide which arrangement works best. In some cases, a simple chronological order is hard to improve upon. Using the five "W's" of journalism could be the best way to organize a jumble of loosely related facts. It should be remembered, though, that the framework of who, what, when, where, and why is designed for news articles, not features. Overuse of this method can make your article easy to follow, predictable - and boring. In a column, as in a feature article, the emphasis should be on unique and novel aspects. Not every fact can be equally important.

Another formula works well for both speakers and writers. It is designed to make an impact upon audience. The key words of the formula go like this:

Ho-Hum!

Who Cares?

Show Me!

So What?

These short phrases remind a speaker or writer to look at his presentation from the audience's point of view. "Ho-Hum" is a reminder that they are not necessarily waiting eagerly for great words of wisdom. The speaker or writer must, first of all, get the attention of the audience completely. Once you have their rapt attention, you must consider their next probable thought, "Who Cares?" Now you must show how your subject, just introduced so brilliantly, personally affects your audience. Why should they care? "Show Me" is a reminder to use specific examples and actual illustrations of your point. These images should be interesting and easy to understand. The final phrase "So What?" tells you to tell your audience what to do about it. Give them a call to action. This formula works because it involves the audience and imparts a definite message. Try it!

If formulas seem too limiting, you can use a less structured method. Start by searching for the essence of your subject. What dominant impression or vivid image sums it all up? Once you have a central theme or a unifying idea, all of the facts and descriptions group themselves around it naturally. Imagine that some freshly felled aspens along a stream inspire you to write about the beavers responsible for this act of vandalism. Your focus could center upon the signs they have left behind. How do their timber-cutting practices differ from a human pulpwood cutter? What is their effect on the environment? How do their construction projects compare to those of human engineers? What tools and equipment do they use? How are these furry engineers outfitted like scuba divers? What does the inside of their lodge look like? How has this animal affected human history? What is its status today? What else do the cuttings bring to mind?

Any one of these questions could serve as a focal point for an entire column, or each question could be touched upon briefly. In any case, there should be one common thread, one idea or image, that ties everything together. It is not necessary to make this thread obvious to the reader or to even state it directly; as long as you keep it in mind, the essence of your subject will come through. Do not lead the reader by the nose; it is better to lead gently.

Clustering

Another metaphoric approach is presented in Gabriele Rico's book, <u>Writing the Natural Way</u>. She recommends that writers use a clustering technique instead of consciously constructing a pattern of organization. Clustering involves writing a single word or topic in the center of a blank sheet of paper and circling it. Then, by using free association, the writer's mind quickly generated related words that radiate from the central word. When you allow the mind to put out a free flow of ideas and words, by writing them down rapidly without judgment or hesitation, an underlying pattern and organizing framework emerges automatically. Here is one example of clustering technique:

Some elements may recur and some may be discarded, but a number of related ideas become readily apparent through this method. It allows you to discover underlying relationships that might otherwise be missed.

Whatever method of organization is used, it should arrange the elements of the subject into a single story or a specific message, one that makes sense to the reader. If outlining works for you, use it without hesitation. If you are able to organize materials by shuffling index cards until the facts arrange themselves in the proper sequence, do it. Organization means putting things into meaningful order. How that should be done is up to you.

If you have difficulty organizing your information, analyze someone else's methods. Study short articles, columns, feature stories and other works to find their underlying structure. Write down the main idea, major themes, the sequence of images, and how different parts work together.

One More Thing

Once you reach the end of your preliminary work of research and organization, your column may be almost written — in your head, at least. However, before you dash off a first draft, check it over, and type up a final copy; it might pay to take one more step — a shuffle draft. This bridges the gap between a basic outline and a first draft; it lets you try out ideas without worrying about how they are written down. To make a shuffle draft, just take each block of information in your outline or arrangement of ideas and expand it with short phrases or a descriptive word or two. Do not try to write in complete sentences or proper style. Use your own personal shorthand, write down ideas with quick abbreviations, jot cryptic notes to yourself to fill out the framework of basic facts you have collected. Do not worry about grammar or syntax. If you hit a snag, move on immediately to another block of information and play with that for awhile. Remember that the more casually you put words down on paper, the easier it will be to eliminate or rearrange them later, if it becomes necessary. It is harder, somehow, to change words that are neatly typed or printed. A shuffle draft will give you a rough sketch of your final sequence of ideas. After that, all you have to do is add the finishing touches.

Running in Circles

One aspect of organization that is commonly found within well-written essays and other shorter writings is the technique of ending at the beginning, or coming full circle. Good writers seem to do this almost instinctively; it is a mark of unified writing that is also pleasing to the reader. Imagine yourself leading your readers on a short guided tour of a small area and returning to the starting point after studying one particular feature. You want your readers to leave with a new awareness and appreciation gained through the experience. Organization and structure are the steps that take them there.

WRITING SAMPLER #2

From Chicago to Dayton, we looked down on a battle, the battle between man's passion for square corners and Nature's penchant for curves.

Across one stretch of country the grid of lines was so accurate, the lines so straight, that I thought that the terrain down there must be as flat as a billiard table, until I noticed that the shadow of our plane was riding humps down there.

It was not only the roads that made squares. The rivets on the wing of the plane were a geometric pattern riding over that geometric pattern down below—a pattern made of fields, and fences, corn rows, woodlots, orchard rows, cemetery plots, and lines of plowing and mowing and irrigation, and sidewalks and driveways of city subdivisions—so uniform that they looked like the product of a punch press.

Under this net, Nature was squirming and resisting.

She was scrawling a meandering zigzag across the ritual of straight lines. And

where a farmer had turned his back for a moment, she was rubbing a thumb across and blurring the precision of impeccable fence rows with a welter of hawthorns, wild plums and wild roses. It was easy to identify the hawthorns from the DC3. There is no mistaking the gray foam of them. And the rest of the fraternity inevitably comes along when the hawthorn invades the fence row.

In one place the farmer's fence had been shifted slightly by an undermining gully.

It could be seen, from this height, that Nature was tampering even with the over-all pattern of man's wheat and rye fields, by overlying the flat squares with a dappled marbling that was sheet erosion.

The pattern of the square is a rare one in living things. Flowers are most often five-parted, less often three-parted and seldom four-parted. It is true, there are some four-parted ones: the mustards, poppies and olives are in fours; and the mints have square stems as do the blue ash and usually the euonymus. But even these squares are softened by flowing contours.

The spiral appears over and over again: in the center of a sunflower head; in the outward corkscrewing of a twig; in the downward thrust of a root tip; in the ascent of a vine. The circle and the five-pointed star are often repeated, the triangle, too. But not the square.

Just when it seemed as if man's geometry was everywhere an alien, temporary mold that had nothing in common with Nature's lines, just then we noticed paths, footpaths that crossed fields near the edge of town, or made a shortcut to a country school or a crossroads community.

These little paths ambled and sauntered. They swung out into curves for no apparent reason. But there must have been a rise of ground, or a depression at each curve, not visible from the air.

Cow paths, too, followed the contour.

Then we saw a country road, dark colored, with edges that were blurred proba-

bly by elderberry, blackberry, bittersweet. It ambled and curved like the little paths. It wandered through a small town, and then, abruptly, it straightened with a jerk, and cut like a gash across a large town. As it entered the outskirts of the town, it passed close to an area marked by a snarl of exaggeratedly curvetting roads and sidewalks, with dark masses of evergreens.

That must have been Suburbia.

From "Looking Down on Improved Property" in Reading theLandscape of America, by May Watts

Unraveling the Threads:

What is your opinion of this selection? Was it easy to follow and understand? Go back and note how her transitions between paragraphs were made. Compare them to the transitions of the first writing sampler. What similarities/differences can you see in their writing style? You may wish to read the complete essay this excerpt was taken from and study it further. You might also read the entire book and analyze the patterns of organization in the rest of the chapters.

The recognition of patterns is an inherent part of May Watts' writing. This particular sample focuses on patterns with the unique perspective of an airborne plant ecologist. It also illustrates principles outlined in the next chapter of this guide. Note especially how she explains complicated and abstract concepts with simple and familiar images.

This excerpt begins with a simple statement of the theme: the conflict between human desires and natural laws. May Watts' vivid images illustrate this theme; the contrasting form of her images reinforce it. Note also how she shifts the vantage point back and forth between the sky and the earth. This increases the impact of her images and involves the reader with her experience. She offers much more than a dry lecture on plant ecology. Her writing always includes the human element.

Her description of a gridwork imposed on a seemingly flat landscape uses the graphic analogy of a billiard table. Straight lines and rigid boundaries work well on a fixed, unchanging surface, she tells us, but they do not fit a dynamic, living landscape.

The image she uses to suggest the hidden complexity of the landscape is the undulating shadow of the airplane. She then compares the rigid pattern imposed on the landscape below with the fabricated metal of the airplane wing. Both have been forced into geometric patterns; the uniform simplicity of the machine has been applied to the land.

The author then gives graphic examples of how nature resists the network of artificially imposed lines. Note how each of her metaphors work in this paragraph, and how plants are used as symbols.

Another single sentence summarizes the effects of viewing a complex, living system in only two dimensions. The summary is symbolized by one small detail of the conflict. Note that she uses "the farmer's fence" instead of the more general phrase "a farmer's fence."

The overall perspective is used again to show that such effects are widespread and general. This more general view leads easily into a discus-

sion of design in nature and in plants. It also repeats her observation that the square is not a natural pattern.

A shift back to ground level suggests that people, too, resist the tyranny of straight lines and squares. We are led down a winding country road softened by the trees and flowers that border it. Suddenly, the road is violently straightened and driven through a larger town. We realize that the plane is nearing the end of its journey and that the essay is also coming to a close. Her straightforward description of her flight serves not only as a vehicle for the organization of her essay, but also as a metaphoric platform for viewing the conflict of man and nature. The experience has ended, but the new perspective she has given us remains.

May Watts typically uses the extended metaphor as a structure for her chapters in Reading the Landscape of America. This technique requires a surprising amount of skill in handling. Extended metaphors used clumsily and without real understanding quickly become trite and pretentious. When used well, though, they leave a lasting impression. Metaphors are valuable tools for the interpretive writer, but they should be used with skill and care.

3

WHO CARES?
Writing for the Reader

Knowledge becomes understanding
when it is coupled with feeling.

-- Alexander Lowen

Language is alive. It is a complex living system that is constantly changing with its environment. The individual words that language is made of must change with conditions as well; it is a rare word that has not changed its meaning or appearance over the centuries. In the 17th century, for example, both *awful* and *artificial* were words of high praise for works of art. Today they could result in a fight between artist and critic. Words may take on a more general meaning over time or they may become more specialized. Both *pigeon* and *pig* originally referred only to the young of both species. A *hound*, on the other hand, used to mean any dog of any breed; now hound is usually reserved to describe a particular kind of hunting dog.

Some words acquire additional meanings that are related to the original sense of the word. Consider how many different ways words like *power*, *head*, or *line* can be used. Some words have a long history of little change; others exist for only a short time before they become little more than curiosities in old books.

Etymology, the study of word origins, allows us to become more aware of subtle shades of meaning; this makes it easier to choose words that express thoughts with precision and accuracy. Since we learn words mostly in the context of passing conversations or casual reading, we may not know their true meaning. Consider *precise* and *accurate*, for example; they do not mean the same

thing. *Precise* means being confined within narrow limits. *Accurate* has the sense of being correct or on target. If you shoot a close grouping of arrows anywhere on a target you are being precise; if you hit the bull's-eye with them you are accurate as well. When words are interchanged carelessly, without regard to their exact meaning, an important distinction is lost.

By studying the origins of words, you develop a feeling for how they best work together. Language cannot be used effectively by someone who does not understand its workings. When you know the precise nature of words, you are less likely to use them in ways that confuse the reader. And unless you fully appreciate the beauty and power of words, you cannot use them to full advantage.

It may be instructive to look at some other word pairs that are often interchanged despite their distinctly different meanings. How well do you know the ones that are listed below?

evidence	proof
mistake	error
inept	clumsy
aggravate	irritate
imply	infer

nauseous	nauseated
disinterested	uninterested
farther	further
tortuous	torturous
regretful	regrettable
presently	currently

You might also consider the words *fame, renown, glory, eminence, repute,* and *notoriety.* Which would you rather have?

Subtle distinctions give words their power of description. Words that overlap slightly in definition can sometimes be exchanged, but every word has a unique history; old meanings and associations cling to new uses and definitions. Study the following words listed as synonyms for *hollow* and note their different senses:

recess, hole, niche, groove, depression, gouge, excavation, cavity, pit, pocket, cup cave, den, burrow

Which one would most likely be made by a bulldozer? Can the word *cavity* be read without immediately evoking images of a dentist? Can a hollow in a tree be called a burrow? Which hollow would shelter a badger, fox, bear, or lichen?

Everyone reacts differently to the same words because of their personal associations. This is especially true of words with general, abstract meanings such as "happiness," "freedom," or "goodness." Tactile, concrete words may also evoke individual impressions, but those impressions are more likely to be felt and shared more deeply. *Oak* creates a much clearer, more definite image in a reader's mind than *tree* does.

By using the word *oak* instead of *tree*, you bring to mind specific characteristics and associations. You may picture a large, spreading tree that casts deep shade with thick, gnarled branches. It is difficult to think of an oak without thinking about its essential and conservative qualities: its solitary and massive presence, its slow, steady growth and long life, and the habit of hanging on to its leaves long after other trees have shed theirs. Strong oak timbers made sturdy floors, furniture, and sailing ships for equally sturdy pioneers.

Because of these and many other associations, the word *oak* itself sounds solid, long-lasting and substantial.

It is also hard to visualize an oak tree without seeing distinctively lobed leaves, swelling acorns with flat caps, or the squirrels that use them. If you have read "The Good Oak" in Aldo Leopold's A Sand County Almanac, you will see saws, tree rings and the way the land used to be. A word like *oak* is packed with a multitude of sharp and vivid images; the word *tree* may contain even more images, but they are too scattered and vague to have much power. Being aware of the impact that words have lets you reach across to a reader. A picture may be worth a thousand words, but one good word can paint a thousand pictures.

Another part of a word's power lies in its sound; even though print is read silently, the sound of words ring inside the reader's mind. Many words have a sound that reinforces their meaning. *Short*, for example, starts with soft, sliding sibilants that are abruptly cut off with hard finality. Words like *short, soft, abrupt,* and *hard* do not imitate the sound that something makes, as *ring* or *buzz* do; they just fit their meaning by their construction. A word like *ugly* makes its meaning apparent to even a person who is unfamiliar with it; note the automatic expression of disgust on your face when you say the word.

Other words have an innately pleasing sound: *sycamore, hush, murmur, melody, tender, lullaby, golden,* and *gossamer.* Words like *burn, slink, dawn,* or *pig* fit their meaning especially well because of their sound and because of our associations with them. When a word has this kind of combination, it has a high impact on the reader.

Many words with high impact have Old English or Anglo-Saxon roots. They are words that were in common use before the influx of French, Latin, and Greek words that began with the Norman Conquest of England in 1066. The majority of the words in the English language today come from these later borrowings; less than twenty percent of our present vocabulary is derived from native English.

Even so, we use that twenty percent much more frequently; of the one thousand most commonly used words, sixty percent have native English origins. They are used frequently because they work well. Native English tends to be earthy and straight-forward; it conveys a simple and direct impression. Some of them, like *tree* or *health* have no adequate substitute.

After a little study and practice, it is easy to recognize these ancient and vital words. See if you can tell which of the following words are derived from Latin and Greek roots and which come from Anglo-Saxon stock.

pendant	hanging
snake	serpent
dig	excavate
walk	amble
perennial	shrub
twig	branch
creeper	vine
liquid	water
seed	grain
percent	share
soil	dirt

Listen to the Anglo-Saxon based words: hanging, snake, dig, walk, shrub, twig, creeper, water, seed, share, dirt. Native English words are not necessarily superior to those we use from Latin or Greek, but it pays to recognize their special qualities.

Why You Can't Just Write the Way You Talk

Writing and speaking may use the same words, but their methods are very different. When you talk to someone standing in front of you, that person is receiving much more than your words. A small pause, a sudden arch of an eyebrow, or the slightest change of tone can completely change the meaning of your words. Think of how many different ways you can express these three simple words: *I will write.*

Stressing any word more than the others alters the intended message. When speaking, you not only have the context to make clear which interpretation is meant, you also have a number of non-verbal cues you can use. In written form the only extra help you have is italics: *I* will write. I *will* write. I will *write.*

Unfortunately, this method of indicating meaning is limited and easily overused to the point where italics lose their effectiveness. A *heavy* use of *any* punctuation mark *for effect* is a *burden* on the reader, *not* a blessing.

Exclamation points, parentheses, dashes, and quotation marks should also be used sparingly; they are seldom necessary. Even though they may make it easier to indicate your "exact" meanings—or show subtle (but significant) nuances of thought—these effects are irritating (and enervating) to the reader! A writer should make the message easy to understand through context and careful choice of wording. Punctuation should be used mainly to emphasize—not to clarify.

With writing, the flow of ideas can go in only one direction, from writer to reader. Besides lacking verbal cues and physical gestures to clarify his meaning, the writer has no way of telling whether the message is being received as sent. The reader cannot display a puzzled expression to the writer or ask how the words are supposed to be interpreted. All the reader can do is read a phrase or passage over again until it becomes clearer—or skip it entirely. The only ways a reader can interpret written symbols are through word order, punctuation, and a native understanding of specific word combinations.

In general, longer sentences need to be more clearly written than short ones because a short sentence is usually easier to grasp or analyze. Reading is a complicated process that requires a great deal of effort. A writer should always try to make the reader's task easier and more enjoyable. Your only rigid rule of writing should be: Help the Reader!

Do not imagine your readers poring over your words of wisdom with eagerness and delight. The people who might be interested in your writing have a great many other things to do. You cannot honestly expect them to seek out what you have to say.

Written messages of all kinds assault our senses and demand our attention all day, everyday. As readers we have learned that most of them are not important; we scan written material quickly to see if it is worth our time and effort. We are not likely to wade through two or three murky paragraphs of introduction on the chance that an article might become interesting.

The Hook

The decision on whether to read an article or not is often made before the end of the first sentence. This is the place to capture the reader's attention; he is under no obligation to discover how interesting (or boring) your material can be.

Here are some opening lines that hook the reader:

> **It began with all the imprecision of a military operation.** (From a column about a Christmas bird count).

> **Sometimes it seems like the whole world is falling apart.** (From an article about bacteria and fungi.)

> **Anyone who doesn't believe in magic hasn't looked outside lately.** (From a column on spring growth.)

> **The man who makes the best pocket-knife in the world is holding mine.** (From an article about Swiss Army knives.)

> **"Those people have to be crazy."** (From another article about Christmas bird counts.)

If your column is buried on a back page, surrounded by glaring headlines and shrill advertisements, you have to make it stand out somehow. Any editor will tell you that pictures are a sure way of attracting attention, especially if they show people or animals. Once they stop to look at an intriguing photograph, readers are likely to read accompanying material that explains it in more detail.

If you are not able to provide suitable photographs on your own, enlist someone else's help. In some cases, drawings or simple graphic illustrations may be better. Whatever illustrations you use, be sure they reproduce well; if you lack experience, contact a graphics specialist. You may want to get one to design a heading for your column that identifies it for your readers. Just remember that your editor must decide what is suitable. Photographs, simple drawings, or a distinctive column heading can attract readers, but you still need to grab them with your first sentence.

How do you do that? An opening question can easily involve the reader, especially if the question is intriguing or disturbing. So can a short dramatic statement that surprises or shocks. You can also start in the middle of your story, at the peak of action, and then go back to explain how you got there. An opening quotation or an obvious play on words can also attract the reader's attention, as will a strange or imaginary situation. The best way to acquire a sense of what will grab your reader's attention is to see how other writers start their articles or essays.

Any opening sentence that hooks the reader should ease that reader into the story before he or she is aware of it. Unless the reader cares what happens next, your hold is tenuous. Once you start, sustain the reader's interest from one sentence to the next, from each paragraph to the next, until you reach the end together.

Keep It Together

Writing reads more smoothly if it has been organized beforehand. Each separate idea or element of the subject should be developed sentence by sentence into paragraphs. Paragraphs are the basic unit of composition; they should flow naturally from one to the next. Transitions between paragraphs should be bridges that are easily crossed, not huge gaps that require long leaps of imagination. Transitions are made easier by letting the second to last sentence of a paragraph set the stage; do not make the last sentence carry the entire load. If your writing has an abundance of stock transitional phrases like *in addition, nonetheless, in conclusion,* and *even though,* you may not be planning your sentences enough. Always look ahead to see how you can bridge the gaps between paragraphs. Anything that interrupts the smooth flow of writing should be eliminated.

Apologies for omissions or shortcomings, for example, may ease your conscience, but they do nothing for the reader except interrupt the flow of thought. Writers with a background in science often interrupt their writing with qualifying statements of conditional phrasing. This type of equivocation is especially jarring to a general audience unfamiliar with it; a reader wants straight facts, not cautious maybes. It is better to simply decide what you want to say, and then say it—without hesitation or equivocation.

Keep It Simple

Reducing the number of modifying phrases, conditional statements and extra descriptions in the middle of sentences also keep your sentences clearer and less confusing. A single sentence can carry only so much information before it collapses under its own weight. Each clause or simple sentence should carry one main thought. When you start a sentence with part of one thought, and then interrupt it with another incomplete thought, you force the reader to hold both incomplete thoughts in mind while he or she tries to figure out how they relate to the rest of the sentence. Reading is a strenuous activity; do not make it even more trying with series of interrupting clauses and phrases that alter the meaning of a sentence.

It is better to complete one long thought before beginning another one. You can never say everything in one sentence; determine for yourself what the reader really needs to know and eliminate unnecessary qualifications or restrictions inside your sentences.

Splitting elements of a sentence that belong together is bound to lead to confusion. A reader will be irritated as well when avoidable interruptions are followed by weak, useless statements.

Of all the insects that teem upon the surface of our earth, including those that buzz in our ears, eat our crops, infest our homes, and generally make our lives miserable, flies are the worst.

Splitting commonly used phrases and constructions is another irritating interruption to be avoided.

"...different in many ways from..."

Here, the expected phrase "different from" is broken up by three extra words that add nothing to the meaning of the phrase.

Dividing verb elements leads to some of the most confusing constructions.

The bluebird has, as a result of unequal competition for nest holes with starlings, among other causes, declined in numbers.

This awkward sentence can easily be rewritten in clearer language by shifting the order of its parts.

Bluebirds have declined in numbers for many reasons, but primarily because of unequal competition with starlings for nest holes.

Perhaps the single best way to avoid confusion and awkward constructions is to keep closely related elements of a sentence as close together as possible. Avoid interruptions in the readers' flow.

Punctuation

Interruptions are a necessary part of writing, of course; shifts in thought and short pauses break up what would otherwise be a monotonous block of print. The spaces between words put them into individual patterns we can recognize. Punctuation organizes the words into coherent groups, a relatively new idea that started with 15th century printers. Punctuation marks are specific signals to a reader that explain the grammatical meaning of sentences.

Periods announce the end of a thought, as well as a sentence. They allow the reader to stop and consolidate the information presented before moving on. Question marks and exclamation points also end sentences, but with a difference. Question marks demand mental responses from the reader and lead the reader to expect a forthcoming answer. Question marks are sometimes forgotten by writers of long convoluted questions. Exclamation points are often overused by enthusiastic writers; they should be reserved for sentences that deserve such special marking. In most cases a period will end a statement with just as much force.

It may seem obvious that periods mark the end of declarative sentences, but they are often misused. Sentence fragments are incomplete statements that lack a verb to go with the subject; they are usually a result of using verbal constructions as nouns or modifiers of nouns in long, complicated sentences. Understandable sentence fragments are sometimes used for effect, especially after questions.

Could this be the source of the blood-curdling noises we had heard last night? The very same.

It was rugged country. Hard. Brutal. Unforgiving. Beautiful.

A little of this goes a very long way. Such fragments usually look better to the writer than they do to the reader. Use them sparingly, if at all.

Elliptical sentences leave out words the reader can fill in without difficulty. They are not considered fragments.

> **The animals (that are) listed as dangerous are not likely to harm anyone (who is) familiar with their habits.**

Overuse of elliptical sentences produces a telegraphic, or headline, style of writing that is ultimately tiring for the reader.

Rambling, run-on sentences, on the other hand, can be pruned and shortened to good advantage with the use of periods. Long, involved clauses can be rewritten into individual sentences that are much easier to swallow. It is a rare writer who uses too many periods. Use the period after a thought has been completed to let the reader pause and reflect before moving on to another thought.

Semicolons;

A semicolon also gives the reader a chance to pause, but it also signals to the reader that what follows is closely related; that is, the second clause explains or amplifies the thought expressed in the first clause. Semicolons make writing read more smoothly by joining ideas that logically belong together. They accomplish this in four different ways:

They separate two main or independent clauses that are not joined by a conjunction.

> **The horses were moving slowly and stopping more frequently; it was obviously time to consider setting up camp.**

They separate main clauses that are joined by conjunctive adverbs.

> **The legislation seemed to be acceptable to all concerned; however, some groups are already trying to change key provisions.**

They emphasize one of three main clauses.

> **The wind dropped, and the clouds parted suddenly; and the moon was shining once again over the water.**

They separate items in a series that require internal commas.

> **Included on the list are sea turtles, the Hawksbill and the Ridley's; sea mammals, the Hawaiian monk seal and the sea otter; and thousands of invertebrate species.**

Colons:

The colon is another punctuation mark that joins ideas. It is used between two main clauses when the second emphatically completes or explains the first clause.

> **We have two choices: fish or cut bait.**

The colon is also used after part of a sentence that introduces lists, explanations, or quotations. It is also subject to overuse.

Dashes—

The dash is a mark used for strong emphasis. It can be used between main clauses when the second, after a dramatic pause, explains the first.

> **The reason is simple—water runs downhill.**

Dashes also set off parenthetical elements that would be separated by commas if they were not inserted for sudden effect.

> **I asked him point blank—and he squirmed as I did it—exactly what was discussed at the closed meeting.**

The dash can also emphasize words added to the end of a complete sentence.

> **The responsibility for this rests squarely on the shoulders of one man—the President.**

Commas,

Commas are subtle cues that tell the reader how a sentence is constructed grammatically. Commas are so vital for indicating the correct interpretation that they should be reserved for that purpose. They should not be inserted as afterthoughts or used just to show the writer's intended emphasis. Commas are an inherent part of a sentence's structure; when used in excess they show a need for rewriting.

Commas separate main clauses joined by coordinating conjunctions (such as but).

The bear was long gone, but I was still frozen in my tracks.

Commas separate and stress parallel clauses that are not joined by coordinating conjunctions.

The sun was up, the birds were wide awake, and I had a whole mountain canyon to explore.

Commas separate the two clauses that make up echo questions.

You don't care, do you?

Commas set off adjective phrase modifiers.

The wood duck, (which was) endangered at the turn of the century, has made a dramatic comeback.

NOTE: The wood duck (that) you missed flew into those trees.

This sentence requires no commas because the modifier refers to a specific case; *that* is used (or understood) to show that an individual duck is meant. *Which* phrases usually require setting off by commas; *that* phrases do not.

Commas set off adverbial phrases at the end of a sentence, especially if it is long or crucial to understanding the thought expressed.

We will eventually realize the extent of the problem, after our aquifers are poisoned.

Commas set off appositive phrases that give examples of the subject.

Many species, such as the black-footed ferret, have never been adequately studied.

Commas clarify introductory adverb clauses used to modify what follows.

Because the problem is so serious, we need your support now.

Commas separate prepositional phrases that need emphasis.

Despite the strenuous efforts of the recovery team, few sea birds survived the oil spill.

Commas set off expressions used for transitions within a sentence.

If we think the battle is over, however, we will once again be caught by surprise.

Commas point out interrupting expressions and phrases.

The real problem, of course, is obvious.

Commas separate words or phrases in a series.

We saw eagles, osprey, cormorants, and sandhill cranes.

Any fixed, unwavering, or endless pattern is extremely irritating.

NOTE: The question of whether or not to use a comma before the word "and" in a series should be answered by considering its value to the reader. In most cases it helps avoid confusion, signals that the last of the series is coming, and emphasizes the final element in the list.

If you try to read any of the sentences used above as examples without the commas, you will see how important commas are to clear writing.

Comma splices are found in sentences with loosely joined ideas. They should be drawn together with a semicolon or a conjunction, or even separated into two distinct sentences instead:

Locally it is considered a minor attraction, and it is visited by people from all over the world.

Some varieties are plentiful, the problem is that we tend to readily overlook anything we call a "weed."

Many states have regulations covering toxic wastes, this isn't one of them.

Since commas and other internal punctuation marks show shifts in thought, they should be used in moderation; excessive punctuation is a sign of complicated writing. However, it is vital that the writer puts in all of the signs the reader needs to find the way.

Casing the Joint

Ideas are joined within sentences by coordinating conjunctions and conjunctive adverbs. A writer should know the specific message each conjunction sends to the reader.

and: **the following idea or clause is equal in importance and structure.**

but: **the following idea or clause modifies what has been stated.**

or: **an alternative or possibility follows.**

for, because: **the next idea or clause supports the first.**

besides, furthermore: **the following ideas or clauses are additional and of equal importance.**

however: **a contrasting or negating idea follows.**

so, therefore: **what was just said will be explained next.**

There are pairs of conjunctions that always appear together:

either...or
neither...nor
both...and
not only...but

and they must be set in the same form of construction when used in a sentence:

***Either* take it *or* leave it.**

That is *both* unkind *and* untrue.

That is *not only* unkind, *but* untrue.

Abbreviations, Contractions and Other Unnecessary Interruptions

Abbreviations save time and effort only for the writer; the reader can scan and read several complete words in less time than it takes to interpret even a standard abbreviation. *Hours* reads more easily than *hrs.*. Ten *seconds* are no longer than ten *sec.* The different meanings of abbreviations for standard Latin phrases such as *i.e.* and *e.g.* are not generally understood; it is better to spell out the English translations *that is* and *for example* instead of using the abbreviations, especially in a text. Even simple and well-known abbreviations like U.S. and NATO are more easily deciphered when they are written in full. A good rule to follow is: "When in doubt, spell it out."

Common contractions such as *don't, aren't, we'll,* and *it's* are useful in imitating speech or for conveying an informal tone, but their use in a column or article should be carefully considered. These contractions do not save the reader any time or make thoughts any clearer. Spelling out these contractions avoids confusion, especially in the case of *it's* and *its.* The reader will not usually notice if verbs are spelled out; have you noticed that contractions are missing from this guide?

Using quotations marks to alter the sense of a word sets up another hurdle for the reader. If you are borrowing a single word from someone else, either say so or simply use the word. Do not use quotations marks to indicate the word does not mean what it says. This "clever" habit is seldom necessary or justified. Do not make the reader guess what you mean.

Vary the Rhythm

Any unchanging, monotonous, unceasing pattern is extremely irritating. Short, choppy sentences may be easy to understand, but they are also difficult to follow. Not all expressed thoughts have equal value; the weight of a sentence should be equal to the thought it expresses. Since a short sentence has the most impact, it should be used to convey thoughts that deserve such special attention. The first statement of a new idea or a summary of what has just been said are good times to use short declarative sentences. Explanations or examples can be more involved.

Fit the Thought to the Sentence

The rhythm of writing is determined by the subject as well as the writer. A series of short staccato sentences may not be the best choice for a description of a peaceful sunrise, but they might work well to evoke the sound of all the birds that go with it. A combination of long, flowing phrases or sentences, set off sharply by short, terse statements might work best to convey the impressions of a whitewater canoe trip. The appropriate sentence structure and rhythm varies with the writer and subject, but it should ebb and flow, like breathing, to fit the situation. Reading sentences aloud will reveal their inner rhythm. Even though writing and reading are separate from spoken language (except perhaps in dialogue) they still leave the sounds of words ringing in our minds.

Emphasis

Emphasis is the basic element of rhythm in both poetry and prose. A writer can gain greater control by understanding the different ways emphasis can be placed. Individual words have emotional and visual impact all by themselves. Certain words like *murder, you,* or *sex* attract the eye immediately and dominate other words in the sentence. A writer should always be aware of the effect individual words may have on the reader. Do not waste strong words on insignificant thoughts or use weak words for important ones.

Take some time to select the right word instead of using one that is merely close in meaning and then adding qualifiers; do not try to make a strong word stronger by piling on adjectives. Phrases like *especially unique, extremely well,* and *completely destroyed* are not only redundant, they are made weaker by the weight of unnecessary words. Modifiers limit meaning, they do not expand it.

Words as well as thoughts can be emphasized by repetition, but this is another technique that should be used with care. Some writers are too careful in this regard, however, and they will write sentences with incredibly convoluted phrasing to avoid repeating a word that recurs naturally in the discussion of a topic. Pronouns are often used to avoid natural repetition in the same way. The result is confusion on all sides.

Otters are members of the mustelid, or weasel, family, as are minks, skunks and badgers. These creatures are noted for their swimming abilities and playful behavior. Although these mammals are familiar to most Americans, few people have actually encountered one of them. It is too bad that such interesting animals are seldom seen in our state today. If you do happen to see one of these delightful relatives of the weasel splashing in a pond someday, consider it a very special experience.

Along with its other glaring faults, this example is hard to follow, mostly because the writer did everything he could to avoid repeating the word "otter."

Emphasis is determined, to a lesser extent, by word order. The most emphatic place in a sentence is at the end. The beginning of a sentence is the next most emphatic position. A short sentence that follows a long sentence is especially emphatic. It has more impact. (The sentences in this paragraph illustrate use of word order and emphasis.)

The internal rhythm of a sentence or a paragraph depends upon the sound of the words chosen and their order of appearance. Repeating consonants, especially at the beginning of neighboring words, is called alliteration. This is a natural expression of rhythm, in fact, it is easy to lapse into alliteration without realizing it. Check over your writing to see if it is being overdone unintentionally. A "flickering flame" may be a cliche, but it illustrates a standard use of alliteration. A "frail flame flickering feebly" overdoes it a bit. Consonants repeated internally are more likely to escape the writers attention, and may lead to a rhythm that is eventually disturbing to the reader. When firefighters "confront a conflagration" or "face a frightening inferno" they also illustrate the overuse of alliteration.

Assonance is the repetition of similar vowel sounds in a sentence or phrase. The words "hedging her bets" show standard assonance; a phrase like "the red shed" rhymes as well. Vowel sounds generally have a pleasing quality, while the sounds of consonants are more likely to leave a harsh, grating impression. A writer should be aware of the sound combinations words create in the reader's mind. Poetry and prose are quite different forms of writing, but an understanding of poetic techniques is a valuable asset for the writer of prose.

Writing should flow naturally, without strain. The reader, however, should not be aware of the methods used to keep things flowing. Anything that draws the reader's attention away from the intended message should be eliminated. Transitional phrases like *Of course, In addition, Consequently, However,* or *Obviously* when used too often to begin sentences reveal a need for better shifts of thought. Phrases like these direct the reader instead of guiding him gently in the intended direction. If your organization is done well, your ideas will follow each other logically. Try to let the second to last sentence of a paragraph set the stage for the first sentence of the next paragraph. Nobody likes being led by the nose; it is better to use subtle transitions than obvious, deprecating and unnecessary phrases like these:

You know, of course...

As you can see...

You are no doubt aware...

Everyone knows that...

By now it should be obvious...

The clear introduction of your ideas—in sentences, paragraphs, articles, or in books—makes it easier for everyone concerned right from the beginning. You should begin and end each paragraph with a significant thought.

Keep It Clear, Simple, and Direct

A strange thing happens to many people when they pick up a pen and begin to write: they suddenly lose the ability to say what they mean. Instead of using words to communicate, they write them in a way that makes communication nearly impossible. It is a common malady among professionals—educators, lawyers, planner, scientists, sociologists and the like—but it seems to especially afflict politicians and bureaucrats. Basically, it requires a person to say as little as possible with as many words as possible. Here are some examples:

A student of Aldo Leopold once wrote the following:

"The scope of this paper has been purposely limited to woody species common to the bear/oak type as it seemed desirable to lay particular emphasis upon the winter season when woody species were not only heavily utilized in general as browse, but were even the sole food of deer following heavy snows."

Leopold translated this as meaning:

"We studied woody plants because deer depend on them in winter, and during snow, may eat nothing else."

From a U.S. government report on the potential effects of nuclear war:

Given the essential inputs which studies indicate would be potentially available to support agriculture needs and current Civil Defense capabilities, sufficient production seems assured to meet survivor needs.

I think this means that if there are any survivors, they will have everything they need to grow food if they have everything they need to grow food.

Those who write this way will not say that people are starving; but they will admit that "their nutritional needs are not being met." They are the same ones who are concerned that the elderly have difficulty "accessing a muffin." (I do not know what it means, either.)

Writing like this has a great many conditional statements and meaningless phrases that hide the meaning instead of making it evident. Nobody is immune to this, of course; all writers seem to lapse into it at times. To write this horrible stuff, it is necessary only to be impersonal, obscure, pompous, evasive, repetitious, awkward, incorrect, faddish, serious, and unintelligible—all at the same time.

Using more words than necessary is another sign of murky writing. Here are some examples, along with their more suitable translations:

...in the case of...	**if**
...as well as...	**besides**
...at one time...	**once**

...in terms of...	in
...on the basis of...	by
...with a view to...	to
...in order to...	to
...would seem to indicate...	means
...as a rule...	does, is
...at that point in time...	then

Some phrases are both pompous and unnecessary:

It is a well-known fact...
One must remember...
In consideration of...
All things considered...

Some overused words or phrases suggest to the reader that what is being said may not even be true. If it is not true, why bother to write it down?

...apparently...
...perhaps...
...possible...
...as far as we know...
...the evidence suggests...
...would seem to indicate...
...usually...
...ordinarily...generally...as a rule...

Some err in the opposite direction:

...really...
...truly...
...very...
...extremely...
...incredible...
...terrific...

High-sounding phrases that say nothing and fancy words that have no meaning are signs of a writer who is not concerned about the reader or interested in providing real information. Qualifying every other statement and maintaining a lofty tone will not make writing objective, any more than gushy, overblown phrasing will make it sincere. Proclaiming false emotion or denying real emotion is not required for sincerity and objectivity; all that is really necessary is a healthy respect for truth.

Parallels and Nonpareils

We are accustomed to seeing related thoughts expressed in similar ways, but an unskilled writer changes forms of phrasing whenever possible, in a mistaken attempt to insert variety. Some of the most memorable thoughts are ex-pressed in parallel form; they are both pleasing to read and easy to comprehend.

First in war, first in peace, first in the hearts of his countrymen.

Give me liberty or give me death.

Put up or shut up.

It is better to give than to receive.

The world will never starve for wonders; but only for want of wonder.

Consider those statements in non-parallel form:

First in war, in the vanguard of peace, and first in his countrymen's hearts.

Give me liberty or let me die.

Put up some money, or don't say anything.

It is better to be the one who gives than to receive.

The world will never starve for wonders; but it may lack people who have wonder.

It is easy to see how parallel structures make ideas easier to follow and understand. This also holds true for articles and prepositions used in a series.

***The* sportsman, *the* landowner, and *the* game warden must deal with the problem together.**

(Try removing one of the articles and see how the sentence is changed.)

...in spring, in summer, in fall, and in winter...

OR...in spring, summer, fall, or winter...

Any disruption of an expected parallel pattern is unsettling to the reader. A good writer realizes the connection between parallel structure and understanding and uses it wherever possible.

Some writers try to create parallels where they do not exist, however, especially with prepositional phrases. Certain phrases that are idiomatic or peculiar to the language do not have to make sense, but they must be followed. If you say, for example, "I have a concern and interest in outdoor recreation," you may imply that you have a business concern or a monetary interest in outdoor recreation. A concern *for* and interest *in* outdoor recreation is an entirely different matter. This may seem like a small matter of form, but distinctions like these are necessary for clear communication. Writing out prepositions or omitting one of the phrases avoids misunderstanding; leaving out a preposition invites it. Knowing which proposition to use with specific phrases requires a native familiarity with the language and its idioms; it cannot be taught.

Part of the power and clarity of parallel structures is a result of keeping related words close together; the position of words in a sentence often determines meaning.

Bathed in sunshine, he found a clearing at the top of the hill.

This would read more easily as:

At the top of the hill, he found a small clearing bathed in sunshine.

Relative pronouns such as *that, who, which,* and *those* should also be kept close to the words they refer to. Any separation can cause confusion; a long separation is almost certain to do so.

The same principle applies to adjectives, adverbs, and modifying phrases. Be aware of the different senses that different word orders imply. The sentences "He only saw two eagles." and "He saw only two eagles." convey entirely different meanings. Rules for placement do not cover all situations, but it is smoother to say, "It has occurred frequently" than to say, "It has frequently occurred." A sentence structure that separates elements that work together is awkward and confusing.

All of the species were not listed.

reads better as:

Not all of the species were listed.

Parallel thoughts in a series are sometimes structured in ways that only seem parallel.

In this century we have conquered tuberculosis, instant communication around the globe and walked on the moon.

On the other hand, writers sometimes try to force unrelated thoughts into parallel structures.

On the advice of the fire department and my engineering staff, the situation was potentially dangerous and we evacuated the building.

Parallel thoughts should also be expressed in the same tense. Shifts from past to present and future are confusing if not made absolutely clear. As native speakers and writers of English, we have an innate good sense of the proper tense to use in simple sentences, even though rules and exceptions to rules are often confusing. Problems arise when we use additional verbs or use them conditionally. A secondary verb does not necessarily follow the tense of the main verb:

Darwin said that natural selection is a constant force.

Changing *is* to *was* in this case would imply that natural selection is no longer a constant force.

Some sentences have a secondary verb that agrees in tense only part way:

He had thought she was alone.

The main problem with using more than one tense in a sentence is the possibility of ambiguity:

He realized that the others had already left and walked back home.

Just who walked home here is not clear. The sentence should read either "...the others had already left for home..." or "...and *he* walked back home." Reading questionable sentences aloud usually makes it clear what needs to be done with them.

Negative Points

Negative words are another potential source of confusion in a sentence or paragraph. Since a second negative cancels the effect of the first one, it is better to use only one negative word in each sentence. Negatives stated in positive form are even clearer; you can say, "He is dishonest" instead of, "He is not honest." The word *not* is a weak and easily overlooked indication of a negative. Substituting other words provides more impact and clarity. "He forgot" is much more direct than "He did not remember."

Conditionals

Conditional forms such as *would, could, may, might,* or *if it were* should be used for situations of real uncertainty. If a possibility or unreal instance is presented in a way that suggests it actually exists, there is a risk of it being taken literally. When a reader is forced to go back to find where the shift was made, it interferes with understanding. Remember that it is easy for a reader to miss single words that change the meaning of sentences; the writer should avoid such situations.

For the same reason, irony, sarcasm, and satire must be handled carefully. Letters to the editor from outraged readers show that some people will always misunderstand tongue-in-cheek statements. This is especially true when such statements are inserted in normal contexts.

A writer cannot expect readers to catch subtle meanings. Once a word or idea is used in a specific way, it should not be changed to indicate something slightly different. Readers are under no obligation to decipher a writer's hidden meanings.

Pronouns

"When I nod my head, hit it with the hammer." This is an example of a pronoun with a vague reference. Although the pronoun *it* is especially open to misunderstanding, any pronoun needs an obvious connection. There are three main ways to avoid using pronouns to confuse the readers.

1. The easiest solution is to simply repeat the original word instead of using a pronoun.

> **First separate whites from yolks and stir them rapidly until smooth.**

These instructions do not tell you whether the whites or yolks should be stirred rapidly. The use of "them" allows the writer to avoid repeating a word, but it confuses the reader. It would be much clearer to say:

> **First separate whites from yolks and stir the yolks rapidly until smooth.**

2. Changing indirect statements to direct statements also avoids confusing constructions. When a sentence like

> **He told them that his lens cap was gone.**

is stated more directly as:

> **"My lens cap is gone," he said.**

the ownership of the lens cap is less ambiguous.

3. By keeping pronouns as close as possible to the word they refer to, you will make your meaning much clearer. This sentence:

> **They invited the engineers because they wanted to hear more about the subject.**

reads more clearly when changed to:

> **Because they wanted to hear more about the subject, they invited the engineers.**

Many awkward and ambiguous constructions are a result of desperate attempts to use correct grammar and maintain a reserved, lofty tone. This results in an overuse of pronouns and the contorted phrases and clauses that often go with them. By writing to inform instead of writing to impress the reader, you will automatically simplify and improve your writing.

Stilted writing uses pronouns when they are not needed:

> **...the fact that...**
> **...which was...which is...**
> **...no doubt that...**
> **...these things are important because they...**
> **...there are many such things that...**

Obscure phrasings can be simplified without any loss of meaning and with a big gain in clarity:

...carries with it...	carries
...the subject of...	use the noun
...fail to remember...	forget
...has the tendency to impart...	gives
...such as those which...	those
...simplistic...	simple

There are certain words that have become meaningless, either because they have been overused to the point of nausea, or because they had little meaning in the first place. Here is a personal selection:

program	facilitate, facility
eventuality	communicate
priority	finalize
prioritize	formulate
inoperative	input, outgo, interface
optimize	insufficiency
mainstream	ball park figure
shortfall	big picture
viable	basically
utilize (for use)	conceptualize
implement	enhancement
absolutely	relate to
verbalize (for say)	speak to that
evaluate	

Add your own choices to the list and keep it as a reminder to use them judiciously in your own writing. You should be especially careful of overusing verbs that end in *-ize* or *-ate* as well as nouns ending in *-ion*.

Every group has its own inside expressions. A *pipe* means something entirely different to a plumber, a musician, or a geologist. These in-group expressions can help individuals in specialized groups and professions define their work more precisely and to work together more efficiently, but some words and phrases serve no real purpose; they merely confuse the issue. Jargon has changed libraries into "media resource centers" and desks into "individualized learning stations." Tax increases have been magically transformed into "revenue enhancements."

People who are enamored with current cliches can never call a spade a "spade." They refer to it as a "garden implement" or an "earth-turning device." The military, which is especially good at this type of thing, once designated the lowly spade as an "entrenchment tool," but this was superseded by the term, "combat emplacement evacuator." By now, the U.S. Army has undoubtedly initiated a new obfuscation.

Newly-coined usages, slang words, and other currently popular additions and foreign borrowings should be used with caution. Although English owes much of its power of expression to new and borrowed words, few are adopted permanently into the language. When you use slang or novel words, you can be certain only that your writing will soon be dated and obscure to many readers. The usefulness of any word or expression depends upon its reception by the reader. It never hurts to use standard and long-accepted language in place of current slang. Whatever your writing may lack in novelty, it will gain in clarity.

Sentence Overloads

Another common cause of murky writing is an overload of adjectives and adverbs. Simple descriptions have more impact than strings of adjectives. It is much easier to feel a "quiet breeze" than a "gentle stirring of cool, moist air moving softly through the dark, leafy shade of the restless trees." It is impossible to squeeze every detail into a description, so put in just the details the reader needs to see the picture.

Ideally, writing should be clear, simple, and easily understood. It should use strong, concise, and unambiguous language that touches the reader. Flowery phrasing has none of these characteristics.

Make It Come Alive

Interpretive writing does more than provide information in grammatical, easy-to-understand language. Interpretive writing involves the reader with images, ideas, and stories that can be shared with words. Here are Freeman Tilden's six principles of interpretation taken from Interpreting Our Natural Heritage and modified slightly for the interpretive writer:

1. Any interpretation that does not somehow relate what is being described to something within the personality or experience of the (reader) will be sterile.

2. Information, as such, is not interpretation. Interpretation is revelation based upon information.

3. Interpretation is an art, which combines many arts, whether the materials presented are scientific, historical, or architectural...

4. The chief aim of interpretation is not instruction, but provocation.

5. Interpretation should aim to present the whole, rather than a part, and must address itself to the whole man rather than any phase.

6. Interpretation addressed to children...should not be a dilution of the presentation to adults, but should follow a fundamentally different approach...

Any definition of interpretation, or interpretive writing, will be incomplete, but one thing is clear: you must *involve* your audience.

Paint Pictures With Words

Do not talk about things; illustrate with real examples. Facts do not speak for themselves; generalities are not easily grasped. Concentrate on seeing images as you write. Imagine the images your words are creating in readers' minds. Instead of discussing birds, talk about robins. Better yet, describe one particular robin that illustrates what you are trying to explain. Abstract concepts stay that way unless they become part of real experiences.

Imagine yourself creating a series of still photographs that will flash across the reader's view as a series of sharp and lasting images. Imagine yourself as a film maker, moving in close to show a crucial detail and zooming back to show the complete picture. Go back in time or move into the future. You can evoke vivid sensations of sights, sounds, smells, tastes, and textures. You can use symbols to stir emotions. But you can do none of these things if you write in generalities that never come down to earth. You have to experience what you are describing in order to share it. Early morning dew, for example, does more than decorate flowers and spiderwebs; it also soaks you to the skin.

Do It, Don't Have It Done

Handbooks on writing invariably tell you to use active voice instead of passive voice, but in fact, both forms have a vital role. Although many writers tend to use passive voice to excess, an uninterrupted series of sentences with subjects acting upon objects and with no subjects being acted upon is unnatural. Passive voice should simply be reserved for situations where you wish to emphasize a passive object more than an active subject.

Those walnuts will be eaten by squirrels before we ever collect them.

(Here the walnuts are the main consideration, not the squirrels.)

Passive voice constructions do not make writing more formal or more proper; they merely shift the weight of a sentence from an active subject to an inactive object. When objects are acted upon instead of acting, they are passive. That is why passive voice is less forceful than active voice. Use it sparingly.

Use Vivid Language

Specific words create distinct images. *Rusty* is more vivid than *brownish-red,* for example. What does a color, shape, or surface remind you of? Go beyond the surface and describe how a thing feels. What details are the most striking? Which are the most basic? Which details are the most surprising? What do they reveal?

If you want to show how trees are part of the hydrological cycle, describe how one tree pumps water from the earth to the air. Better yet, tell how the maple in your reader's yard pulls thousands of gallons of water into the sky above his house. Show how it works like a giant air conditioner to cool it. Describe how that coolness feels on a hot day. Tie that maple tree in with all of the other green plants that cool and cleanse the earth. Make connections with real images.

Analogy, Simile, and Metaphor

When you use a particular example to describe something else that is similar in structure or function, you are using an analogy. When you say it acts or looks like something else, you are using a simile or metaphor. Similes and metaphors present things that are different as if they were alike. Perhaps it is this paradoxical nature that gives analogies and metaphors their creative impact.

Similes retain a slight distinction between compared objects by using *like* or *as* in their construction.

My love is like a red, red rose.

He's as jumpy as a long-tailed cat in a room full of rocking chairs.

Metaphors relate two separate images that would not normally be considered together without the distinguishing words "like" or "as." The power of a metaphor lies in the sudden recognition of an unexpected similarity.

Weeds are Nature's band-aids; they protect wounds in the earth's skin and help them heal.

Many words are fossil metaphors. *Translate* literally means to "carry across." The word *depend* comes from Latin "to hang from." The word *tap* originally meant "a light blow"—the kind you would use to "tap" a wooden keg or barrel. Later the meaning attached itself to the device that tapped the barrels' contents. Further expansion of meaning allowed the "tapping" of resources of any kind— and a multitude of other metaphors.

An extended or a false analogy lacks impact and misses the mark because it has only a superficial connection. An automobile may need fuel and it may start sluggishly on cold mornings, but it is an oversimplified analogy to the human body. Extended analogies fall apart when they are stretched too far.. If you do ever use one, leave it subtle and unstated. Using a single analogy as a framework for an entire column or article requires a great deal of skill and handling. Such cleverness usually pleases the writer much more often than it does the reader.

Symbolism uses a part to represent the whole, a process called synedoche. A recurring symbol is a solid reference point for a reader exploring a complex subject. A writer who returns to a central image at each shift in direction or development will give the reader a more cohesive view of the subject.

Any structure or device used for effect should be used to enhance communication, not the writer's esteem. Tricks and techniques that are too obvious or that strain the written message to fit an artificial structure do not help the reader. An old bit of advice on this matter suggests that if a phrase, metaphor, or sentence seems especially well written, it should be taken out immediately because it will only distract the reader's attention from the intended message.

Leave Something to the Imagination

Do not try to explain or tell everything. Let the reader fill in conclusions from the pertinent facts. It is much more fun to discover things on your own than to have someone tell you everything. Involvement is again the key element here. Overdoing clever phrases, cute metaphors, or novel forms tend to separate reader and writer, instead of bringing them together.

Relate

Whenever possible, relate your images, ideas, and symbols to familiar objects in the reader's experience. This concept has been mentioned here more than once, but relating the unfamiliar to that which is already known is such an important aid to understanding that it deserves mention in more than one context.

People relate more easily to other people than to other things. Animals and plants that remind us of ourselves are always more fascinating than those that don't. That is one reason cartoon animals are perennial favorites; they act like we do. Cute furry creatures that nurture their young and walk on their hind legs have more appeal than cold-blooded reptiles or mindless insects. By showing shared qualities or similar actions, you make it easier for the reader to relate to your subjects.

Contrast

Similarities tie things together, but contrast makes them stand out from their background. You can make images more distinct by highlighting contrast. A soft delicate fern is made even more so by a niche of raw, exposed rock. The fleeting light of a firefly is even more impressive against a backdrop of distant stars. One flower, appreciated in detail become even more amazing when seen as one individual in a whole field of flowers.

Looking at things in terms of both similarities and differences gives a much better picture to the reader. Deal with the universal as well as the particular.

Style

Your style as a writer is a reflection of your particular background and personality. A regular column allows you to project yourself into your writing more than other formats. Regular readers enjoy their vicarious relationship with a writer whose work they enjoy. The writer of a column can inject personal thoughts and views more readily than with an article, but this privilege should not be abused.

A regular column also demands that the writer have a consistent style. This does not mean that new approaches or a different type of subject should not be used; it means that the reader should always find what he expected—and more. This is easier to do if you choose interesting topics and keep a good sense of curiosity. The more you learn and experience, the more interesting things you will have to write about.

Read!

If you want to be a good writer, you have to be a good reader. Reading widely is essential to learning how to use language to express thought. Reading gives you information and an understanding of how to use it.

Study other writers' work; see how they arrange words and ideas to create art. Determine for yourself what makes writing good or bad. What specific qualities can you find in writing you consider especially enjoyable? Read handbooks of English usage and volumes of poetry. Read columns and essays with special attention. Read over books by classic nature writers for inspiration as well as instruction. Read about things outside the field of natural history; if everything really is connected to everything else, you will use *any* information you find to good advantage.

WRITING FOR THE READER: A SUMMARY

- **Experience.**
- **Read.**
- **Involve the reader.**
- **Relate your subject to familiar things.**
- **Show, don't tell.**
- **Describe action, don't talk about ideas.**
- **Use words to create images and impressions.**
- **Avoid false objectivity and overblown imagery.**
- **Be sincere.**
- **Use details that reveal the whole picture.**
- **Show connections.**
- **Unify your writing with a central image or theme.**
- **Describe real people, experiences, and things.**
- **Be clear, simple, direct, and unambiguous.**
- **Take the time to find the right words.**
- **Use moderation in all things.**
- **Help the reader.**

WRITING SAMPLER #3

Well — the sun will be up in a few minutes and I haven't even begun to make coffee. I take more baggage from my pickup, the grub box and the cooking gear, go back in the trailer and start breakfast. Simply breathing, in a place like this, arouses the appetite. The orange juice is frozen, the milk slushy with ice. Still chilly enough inside the trailer to turn my breath to vapor. When the first rays of the sun strike the cliffs I fill a mug with steaming coffee and sit in the doorway facing the sunrise, hungry for the warmth.

Suddenly it comes, the flaming globe, blazing on the pinnacles and minarets and balanced rocks, on the canyon walls and

through the windows in the sandstone fins. We greet each other, sun and I, across the black void of ninety-three million miles. The snow glitters between us, acres of diamonds almost painful to look at. Within an hour all the snow exposed to sunlight will be gone and the rock will be damp and steaming. Within minutes, even as I watch, melting snow begins to drip from the branches of a juniper nearby; drops of water streak slowly down the side of the trailer house.

I am not alone after all. Three ravens are wheeling near the balanced rock, squawking at each other and at the dawn. I'm sure they're as delighted by the return of the sun as I am and I wish I knew the language. I'd sooner exchange ideas with the birds on earth than learn to carry on intergalactic communications with some obscure race of humanoids on a satellite planet from the world of Betelguese. First things first. The ravens cry out in husky voices, blue-back wings flapping against the golden sky. Over my shoulder comes the sizzle and smell of frying bacon.

That's the way it was this morning.

From Desert Solitaire by Edward Abbey

Unraveling the Threads

How does this piece differ from the other samples? What features does it share with them? Did you enjoy reading it? Which of the samples do you feel most comfortable with? Do you know why? How does this sample illustrate the points brought up in the last chapter? Good writers have a distinctive, easy to recognize style. What are the basic elements of Abbey's style? Read his book Desert Solitaire and note how Abbey involves the reader. Compare his techniques with those of the other writers excerpted for this guide.

Edward Abbey's writing is well-suited to the desert landscapes he describes so fondly. It is simple and direct, with clear, expressive, and colorful images. Abbey is also intensely personal; he states his thoughts freely, with dry caustic wit. Because he is so straightforward, there are few embellishments. A reader has little difficulty knowing exactly what Abbey is talking about. A spare and lean writing style does not necessarily mean that the writing lacks substance or depth,

however. There is a wealth of understanding behind simple, well-chosen words.

A piece of writing can hold messages at many different levels of understanding. Many of our best-known fairy tales, for instance, are thinly-disguised attacks on the establishment of their day. Regardless of the levels of meaning included, however, the basic story must be able to stand on its own merits. Hidden meanings and symbolic images can be incorporated into the story for discerning readers, but they should never get in the way of a good story. Too many writers show a lack of subtlety.

This excerpt shows how Abbey uses written imagery and an unadorned style to involve his readers in the experiences he describes. Note how the opening line gives a sense of calm excitement and anticipation. By tying the warming sun and his morning coffee together, he joins the familiar and close-at-hand with the mysterious and far-away. His short, vivid description of simple needs are made of well-chosen words. His images of frozen food and frozen breath heighten the anticipation of the approaching sunrise. The rhythm of the sentences reinforce the feelings he evokes.

As he steps out with a cup of steaming coffee, "hungry for the warmth," the reader is also drawn outside, waiting for the sun. The images of warmth and light come quickly, in a long rush of descriptions. Familiar frameworks of walls and windows and towers heighten the impression of being in a strange, mysterious setting. The picture of Abbey and the sun greeting each other across the gulf of 93 million miles make the sun seem more personal, even as it remains awesome and unimaginably distant. There is also a sharp contrast in the images of cold, hard snow sparkling in the warmth of the sun. Snow melting into running water adds motion and life to the setting.

The sudden appearance of three ravens snaps the reader from the quiet reverie. Mystery is evoked again with the line, "I am not alone after all." Abbey suggests that there are immense distances to be traversed on earth as well as in space. Birds are contrasted nicely with imaginary aliens.

The sentence "First things first." puts everything in perspective. The birds fly against the desert sky and breakfast is waiting on the stove. That's the way it was that morning; the reader is sure of that. Edward Abbey has described a simple, earthy experience and given it cosmic connections. You don't have to read it that way, though. All you have to do is enjoy the experience.

4

THEN YOU JUST CUT AWAY EVERYTHING THAT DOESN'T LOOK LIKE AN ELEPHANT...
Rewriting and Revising

I would have written you a shorter letter, but I didn't have the time.

— Mark Twain

Ideally, your final draft should be so well-crafted and tightly woven that no single part can be changed without changing everything else. In reality, your writing can always be changed for the better. As a writer, you know exactly how your words should be understood. The reader, however, cannot read your mind, just the words you put on paper. Revising and rewriting means making sure that the reader gets the message you think you are sending. It is your last chance to get your words down right. to do it, you must look at your writing objectively, one of the hardest parts of the job.

If you can put a little time and distance between yourself and what you have just written, it will be much easier to look at it later with a fresh and critical eye.. If you have ever discovered an old school composition after a few years of neglect, you already know how time gives a clearer perspective. Even if you have only a short time available before your deadline, leave your writing alone for a while. Let it sit before you attempt to edit it.

A professional editor can offer pertinent advice and valuable assistance, but do not expect the newspaper or magazine editor you are writing for to do your work. An editor's job is to make minor corrections in copy, not rewrite it.. Do as much as you can to make the editor's job an easy one; find out what standards and practices are in force before you submit your copy.

If you give your writing to a non-professional for criticism, that person is not likely to have the background and ability to make specific corrections as they are needed. Friends and acquaintances do not like to be critical, anyway. They will also tend to notice mostly the things that differ in style from their own writing. However, they can still help you out if you ask them more specific questions than "What do you think?" You should ask them questions like these:

Where did you have to slow down?

Where did you have to stop and go back to understand what was said?

Which parts do you remember?

What could be left out?

Which parts were confusing?

What do you think the main idea or message is?

Even if you do not have a hard-hearted editor or a critical friend available, you can look at your own writing with more objectivity by using simple editing techniques.

Try reading your writing as quickly as possible. This will show you where the seams are still ragged in your composition. The places that cause you to stumble are likely to do the same thing to your readers. Try reading it aloud, in a monotone. By leaving out voice inflections that you know are there, you will come closer to the situation of your readers, who do not. If you attempt to intentionally misread what you have written, you will find it easier to spot ambiguous phrases and misleading constructions. Look for places where a missing word or two would make things clearer. Ask yourself what kind of impression your writing will give to the reader. Do you seem sincere and straight-forward? Aloof? Equivocating? Flippant? Patronizing? Boring?

If the rhythm of your writing seems choppy and disjointed, smooth out your transitions. Try simpler and smoother phrasings. Check for excessive punctuation. Are there pauses between ideas? Are they too long or too short? Does your rhythm flow with your subject's pace and mood? Remember that reading aloud brings out the rhythm. Check for run-on sentences, sing-song phrasing, and unintentional overuse of alliteration.

Look at individual words to see if they say what you really mean. Synonyms rarely ever mean the same thing. See if you can replace fancy words with simple ones. Try to replace multiple verb forms with single verbs. Be sure pronouns are clear in their relationships. Seek out any mixed metaphors or tangled analogies. Determine if the amount of words spent on each part of the topic is equal to that part's importance. See if an especially striking phrase is merely calling attention to itself instead of helping to send the message.

Be sure your ending is as strong and clear as your opening; do not end your article by fading into banalities. Look for words, phrases, and paragraphs that are just filling space in the middle of your column. Do you come to the point without beating around the bush? It is always easier to say too much about something than it is to say too little.

Danger Signals

When you return to your work look for these signs of trouble; they will point out elements that may need rewriting:

1. *So that...*

   Use *because* instead.

2. *... there are...(things) which...*

   Write either *many (things)*...or use specific adjectives.

...that are, which is, and *that was* should also be avoided.

3. *...has as...*

   Try using *is* instead.

4. A sentence beginning with *However...* or *Also...*

   This may inadvertently shift the emphasis from the major thrust of the sentence.

5. *...useful...important...critical...interesting*

   Words like these are seldom any of the above. See if the sentence is necessary.

6. An uninterrupted series of short words.

   If each word is grammatically necessary to convey the meaning, the reader can easily miss one and misinterpret the sentence. A long series of short words is often a sign of complicated grammar.

7. A series of *ofs*

   These confusing phrases can usually be replaced by single adjectives. Use more specific language.

8. An unbroken series of nouns

   When words normally used as nouns are strung together, all but one of them are really being used as adjectives. This forces the reader to shift his interpretation after each one.

   It is a brick facade tract house neighborhood.

9. Double negatives

   Double negatives are confusing. Use only one negative in a sentence.

10. Abbreviations

    When in doubt, spell it out.

11. Too many hyphenated words

These shortcuts can often be written more clearly in other ways.

12. Too many words that end in *-ion, -ate,* or *-ize*

13. *...the latter...the former...* OR *first,...second,...third...*

Do not make the reader go back to check relationships in a list. Repeat the name or division you are referring to. Also, avoid *secondly, thirdly,* and the like, unless you plan to use phrases like *Firstly...*

14. *Such* used as a pronoun

Such usage is always confusing and/or pompous. Repeat the noun.

15. *...and which...*

This construction does nothing but get you into trouble.

16. Saying the same thing in different words; repeating a thought for no particular reason

17. Floating pronouns: *which...that...they...who...these...those...*

18. A lot of words ending in *-ly*

Overqualifying is limiting.

19. Gerunds, participles, and infinitives

Verbal constructions used as nouns can be easily misused; check them carefully to see if they agree with the rest of the sentence.

20. Excessive punctuation

21. Cliches

Avoid them like the plague. If you do use them, do not try to rewrite them.

When you find gaps, hitches, or snarls in your writing, ask yourself the following questions:

-Which words are closely related to each other? Are they close to each other in the sentence?

-Which clause holds the main thought? Is it the main clause?

-What is the subject of your main thought? What is the grammatical subject?

-Would active voice be smoother and clearer than passive voice?

-Can an awkward sentence be made into two or more sentences? Should it be combined with another sentence?

-Can interrupting clauses or phrases be moved to in front of the main subject or after the main clause?

-Does the main verb carry the main meaning or action?

-Does every word do a job?

-Does each preposition fit the object word it is placed with?

-Can a more specific word replace a string of adjectives and the word they modify?

-Which modifying phrases can be shortened by removing unnecessary words? Could they be eliminated entirely?

-Should a "which" be changed to a "that" to show that the clause it introduces is vital to the meaning?

-Does a sentence seem to need more adjectives or clauses to become clear in meaning? Perhaps it should be developed into a full paragraph.

-Would the missing words in an elliptical clause make the sentence easier to understand if they were put in?

-Are "a," "an," and "the" used properly?

Try alternate constructions and phrasings in your head or on an extra sheet of paper before changing your copy. Whenever possible, write sentences that are short, simple, clear, and direct.

Sentence length should vary, of course, but an average length of 15 words is a good guide to follow. Rudolf Flesch, in his book <u>The Art of Readable Writing</u>, suggests counting the number of sentences in a 100-word sample as an index to readability. He says the average sentence length should range form less than eight words to no more than 17 words. He also recommends that the average number of syllables in a 100-word sample should range from less than 123 to a maximum of 147 syllables. For a more complete explanation of Flesch's system, you must refer to his book. Flesch has found that most writing, even in popular magazines and books, is too complicated to be readily understood by the average reader.

Of course, a reader enjoys being mentally challenged on occasion, and new concepts often require the use of new words. The easiest way to introduce new words is with appositives, or parenthetical definitions set off by commas.

These daily behavior patterns, or circadian rhythms, are an intimate fact of life.

Remember, also, that readability is not determined by sentence length alone. If the omission of certain words leads to confusion or ambiguity, readability suffers. Concentrate on removing unnecessary modifiers and clauses; the telegraphic writing style in many advertisements, magazines, and newspapers can be misunderstood unless sentences are kept short and strictly parallel. A reader can scan a long sentence that is clearly written much faster than he can decipher a short sentence with a confusing construction.

Revising and rewriting does not mean wholesale changes in subject matter or organization; it means putting the final touches on a finished product. If editing seems too difficult, it may be because of incomplete planning and organization instead of faulty writing alone. Once your first draft is done, you must decide if it says exactly what you want to say, as simply as you can say it. Editing means taking out anything that gets in the way. Just be sure that any changes you insert into a sentence or paragraph do not interrupt the original flow of your writing.

Whenever possible, read good writing and study it with a critical eye. This will give you a better understanding of both writing and rewriting.

WRITING SAMPLER 4

The cattail is one of the most interesting and oldest plants of the wilderness. A cattail grows eight or ten feet in one season, sending up a straight stem with a brown cylinder near its top that looks like a big sausage on a spit. Around this, long, slender leaves form circles and curves that never stop dancing. One big brown "sausage" is made with a half million flowers pressed closely together, and each flower produces a seed too small for the eye to see.

From one of these invisible seeds falling into the mud of the swamp a stem grows sideways, not up like the stems of ordinary seeds. This stem is so filled with energy that in a few days it may be several feet long and putting out branches in all directions. Where these branches touch, they join each other so that a net of stems is woven horizontally through the mud at the bottom of the swamp.

A single cattail plant may spread its branches through three acres of swamp.

It was these under-mud stems which the Indian masters had forced the slave Cabeza to dig up. This was a tough and bloody job, and the Spaniard who thought of good food in terms of the fruits and spicy dishes of Spain never realized that the "roots," as he called them, were nourishing food.

Those under-mud cattail branches are not made of wood. They are filled with air and a pulpy substance that has as much nourishment as corn, rice, and potatoes. The stems are enclosed in a waterproof covering so that this food and air may be buried in the mud underneath water that is stale or salty and yet keep as fresh as though in cold storage. This big system for self-contained air

and food enables the cattail to live if the swamp dries up and keeps it from suffocating in deep water if there is a flood. The buds on its stems buried in the bottom of the swamp can open, and, with the energy of food from below and its internal air supply, their shoots can grow up through eight feet or more of water to thrush their sausages up into the air sunshine.

And those slender, curving leaves are hurricane-proof. Instead of a framework of lengthwise veins, the leaves have a series of crosswise girders, like the wing of an airplane. such a leaf can be whipped in any direction without tearing. When a hurricane strikes a cattail swamp, the leaves fend the force of the blow by flowing in the wind, while the spikes bend over and bury themselves in the water. When the storm is spent, the spikes snap back to an erect position and the leaves gently rise, describing their circles and curves as though nothing had happened.

- Excerpt from <u>Wilderness</u>
by Rutherford H. Platt

Unraveling the Threads:

Since this writing sample is an excerpt, the organization of the chapter it was taken from is not apparent. For example, the reference to the Spanish explorer Cabeza in the third paragraph works as a unifying image for the chapter. A more com-

plete reading is necessary for an accurate assessment of Platt's writing.

How would you compare this sample with the others in this guide? Is it interpretive writing or just factual reporting? What makes you think so? By now you should be reading with a more critical eye. Edit and rewrite any parts of this sample that you think should be changed to help the reader. Are the necessary changes major or minor in nature? After you have analyzed Platt's treatment of cattails, try writing your own article about cattails, in the same number of words, using any approach you like. When you are finished writing and editing your article, compare it with Platt's. If you were an editor, which one would you select for publication? Get a second or third opinion. Try doing the same thing with the other samples.

You can also try to write articles that mimic the style of other writers. For instance, you could relate the essence of autumn in the style of Mary Leister. You could recreate a drive across the countryside as May Watts would, or describe a sunset you have experienced in the manner of Edward Abbey. Exercises like these will give you a clearer understanding of the writing process and help you to develop your personal writing style. Read the works of other authors listed in the Appendages. Good writing can be read many times, for instruction as well as pleasure. The idea is not to write like someone else, but to learn from as many different sources as you can and blend what you find into a new experience for your readers.

5

WHAT YOU SEE IS NOT WHAT THEY GET
Preparation for Print

Oh wad some power the giftie gie us
To see oursels as others see us!

- Robert Burns

Once you have met the challenge and overcome all obstacles in your path, you are ready to go into print. Whether you write with pen and paper or on a keyboard, find out what happens to your copy after you submit it for printing. Get to know the people and processes that are involved; it will make things easier for everyone concerned.

First of all, be sure your copy is as complete and accurate as you can make it. If it is submitted on typed sheets, have it double-spaced with wide margins so the editor can insert corrections and directions. Any last-minute changes you make on your submitted copy should be minor ones, like transposed letters or missing words. Do not try to rewrite sentences or rearrange paragraphs on the copy you hand in for printing. Make your corrections between the lines; margins should be reserved for the editor and the person setting your copy. Know the standard proofreading symbols and what they mean. Know how to properly indicate italics, underlining, numbers, and symbols. Identify and number any photographs or drawings on the reverse side with a soft-lead pencil.

Be sure to meet your deadlines. When you are late with your copy, there is less time to find errors and correct mistakes. You will also be holding up the entire printing operation if you bring your copy in late. You should also remember that your writing will look different when it finally appears in print. A short paragraph looks much longer when it is double-spaced on typing paper or when it appears on a screen. Consider how your column will be made up with the rest of the page. Keep each column to a reasonable, standard length.

The right word processing program can save you a great deal of time and effort in preparing articles for print. You still have to provide the creativity, of course, but word processors can help you transform it into print. There are a wide array of writing programs to choose from. Some will help you build up an organizing outline from scratch, correct your spelling automatically, give you an immediate listing of a word's synonyms, or even tell you when you are using a word or phrase too often. Some can call attention to errors in punctuation, suggest alternatives to pompous phrases, or come up with the word that you have right on the tip of your tongue. If you have access to a word processor, it would pay to check into the possibilities. Ask other writers which programs they have found most useful and go over reviews of word processing programs and their capabilities to see which one best fits your needs. Try several out before making an investment in a particular package.

Perhaps the biggest benefit of a word processor is the ability to see your ideas in print immediately. This allows you to review your writing as you go along, something that takes a lot longer when you write or type on paper in between corrections.

Columns and articles in newspapers and magazines are often written in essay form, a demanding type of writing that demands tight organization and practiced skill with words. It requires that you write only what is necessary to your topic and no more. Rambling disjointedly in a hundred different directions with no particular purpose will not do. Your writing must be sharp and to the point, with no extra words. This is difficult to do, but it is also immensely satisfying when you do it. You will find it easier if you remember:

Don't worry about what you are writing; worry about what they are reading.

Enjoy yourself!

REFERENCES

Chapter One

Express Yourself In Writing
Gail Kledenser
Sterling Publishing Co., 1968

Proper Words In Proper Places
Irving T. Richards and Paul I. Richards
The Christopher Publishing House, 1964

Words On Paper
Roy H. Copperud
Hawthorn Books, 1980

Word Power Makes the Difference
Duane G. Newcomb
Parker Publishing Co., 1975

Writing the Natural Way
Gabriele Lusser Rico
Tarcher Books/Houghton-Mifflin Co., 1983

Chapter Two

The Art of Readable Writing
Rudolf Flesch
Harper and Bros., 1949

The Careful Writer
Theodore Bernstein
Atheneum, 1978

D.C. Dialect
Paul Morgan and Sue Scott
Washington News Press, 1975

The Elements of Style
William B. Strunk and E.B. White
Macmillan Publishing Co., 1979

English As Language: Backgrounds,
Developement, and Usage
Ed. by Charlton Laird and Robert Gorell
Harcourt Brace Publishers, 1961

Express Yourself In Writing
Gail Kledenser
Sterling Publishing Co., 1978

Interpreting Our Heritage
Freeman Tilden
Univ. of North Carolina Press, 1977

On Writing Well
William Zinsser
Harper and Row, 1980

Origins: A Short Etymological Dictionary of Modern English
Eric Partridge
Greenwich House, 1983

Our Marvelous Native Tongue: The Life and Times of the English Language
Robert Claiborne
Times Books, 1983

Proper Words In Proper Places
Irving T. Richards and Paul I. Richards
The Christopher Publishing House, 1964

Simple and Direct: A Rhetoric for Writers
Jacques Barzun
Harper and Row, 1975

The Ways of Language: A Reader
Ed. by Raymond Pflug
The Odyssey Press, 1967

Word Power Makes the Difference
Duane G. Newcomb
Parker Publishing Co., 1975

Writing the Natural Way
Gabriele Lusser Rico
Tarcher Books/Houghton Mifflin, 1983

Chapter Three

The Art of Readable Writing
Rudolf Flesch
Haprer and Bros., 1949

The Elements of Style
William B. Strunk and E.B. White
Macmillan Publishing Co., 1979

<u>Express Yourself In Writing</u>
Gail Kledenser
Sterling Publishing Co., 1978

<u>Proper Words In Proper Places</u>
Irving T. Richards and Paul I. Richards
The Christopher Publishing House, 1964

APPENDAGES

The books listed in the Appendages that follow are only a sampling, to be enjoyed at random. That is why they are not listed alphabetically or ranked in any order. The list is also incomplete, of course. It is impossible to include every useful or deserving book. You will undoubtedly be familiar already with many of the titles; others may have escaped your notice. You are invited to add your own discoveries and selections to each category. You will then have a personal — and more comprehensive — list of recommended reading that you can share with anyone else who shares your interests.

Asterisks (*) mark titles and/or authors I have found especially useful and/or well-written.

Handbooks on Writing:

The Careful Writer
Theodore Bernstein
Athenum, 1978

Simple and Direct
Jacques Barzun
Harper and Row, 1975

Words on Paper
Roy H. Copperud
Hawthorn Books, Inc., 1980

The Art of Readable Writing
Rudolf Flesch
Harper and Brothers Publishers, 1949

Express Yourself In Writing
Gail Kredenser
Sterling Publishing Co., Inc., 1968

Word Power Makes the Difference
Duane G. Newcomb
Parker Publishing Co., Inc., 1975

*Proper Words In Proper Places
Irving T. Richards and Paul I. Richards
The Christopher Publishing House, 1964

Writing the Natural Way
Gabriele Lusser Rico
Tarcher Books/Houghton Mifflin Co., 1983

*The Elements of Style
William B. Strunk and E.B. White
Macmillian Publishing Co., Inc., 1979

*Interpreting Our Heritage
Freeman Tilden
The University of North Carolina Press, 1977

*On Writing Well
William Zinsser
Harper and Row, 1980

Reference Books for Writing:

Bartlett's Familiar Quotations
Edited by Emily Morison Beck
Little, Brown, and Co., 1980

The New Roget's Thesaurus in Dictionary Form
Edited by Norman Lewis
Berkley Books, 1981

*Dictionary of Word Roots and Combining Forms
Donald J. Borror
Mayfield Publishing Co., 1960

Words Into Type
Marjorie E. Skillin
Prentice-Hall

The Dictionary of American Bird Names
Ernest A. Choate
Gambit, 1973

Books on Words and Language:

Words
Paul Dickson
Delacorte Press, 1982

English As Language; Backgrounds, Development, and Usage
Edited by Charlton Laird and Robert Gorell
Harcourt Brace Publishers, 1961

*Our Marvelous Native Tongue
Robert Claiborne
Times Books, 1983

A Browser's Dictionary
John Ciardi
Harper and Row

Origins; A Short Etymological Dictionary of Modern English
Eric Partridge
Greenwich House, 1983

The Ways of Language: A Reader
Edited by Raymond Pflug
The Odyssey Press, Inc., 1967

Stars and Planets:

The Stars; A New Way to See Them
H. A. Rey
Houghton-Mifflin Co., 1976

The Night Sky Book; An Everyday Guide to Every Night
Jamie Cobb
Little, Brown, and Co., 1977

Reasons for Seasons; The Great Cosmic Megaglactic Trip Without Moving From Your Chair
Linda Allison
Little, Brown, and Co., 1976

A Field Guide to the Stars and Planets
(The Peterson Field Guide Series)
Donald H. Menzel
Houghton-Mifflin Co., 1964

Atmosphere, Weather, and Climate:

A Field Guide to the Atmosphere
(The Peterson Field Guide Series)
Vincent J. Schaefer
Houghton-Mifflin Co., 1981

Weather Wisdom
Albert Lee
Doubleday and Co., 1976

Weather
(A Golden Science Guide)
Paul Lehr, R. Will Burnett, and Herbert S. Zim
Golden Press, 1965

Geology, Landforms, Rocks and Minerals, Fossils:

A Guide to Field Identification: Rocks and Minerals
Charles A. Sorrel
Golden Press, 1973

Landforms
(A Golden Science Guide)
George F. Adams and Jerome Wyckoff
Golden Press, 1971

Fossils
(A Golden Field Guide)
Frank H. T. Rhodes, Herbert Zim, and Paul R. Schaffer
Golden Press, 1962

Water:

*The Infinite River; A Biologist's Vision of the World of Water
William H. Amos
Random House, 1970

*The Sea Around Us
Rachel Carson
Oxford University Press, 1950

Life and Death of the Salt Marsh
John and Mildred Teal
Ballantine Books, 1969

A Field Guide to the Atlantic Seashore
Kenneth E. Gosner
Houghton-Mifflin Co.

Pond Life
(A Golden Field Guide)
George K. Reid
Golden Press, 1967

Bacteria and Fungi:

Magnificent Microbes
Bernard Dixon
Athenum, 1976

Mushrooms of North America
Orson K. Miller, Jr.
E.P. Dutton, 1978

The Mushroom Hunter's Field Guide
Alexander H. Smith
University of Michigan Press, 1963

Mushroom of the Great Lakes Region
Verne O. Graham
Dover Books

The Mushroom Handbook
Louis Krieger
Dover Books

Non-Flowering Plants: Ferns, Mosses, Liverworts, and Club Mosses:

How to Know the Ferns
Frances T. Parsons
Dover Books

A Field Guide to the Ferns
(The Peterson Field Guide Series)
Boughton Cobb
Houghton-Mifflin Co.

Ferns of the Northeastern United States
Farida A. Wiley
Dover Books

Fern Finder
Anne C. Hallowell and Barbara G. Hallowell
Nature Study Guild, 1981

Non-Flowering Plants
(A Golden Field Guide)
Floyd S. Shuttlesworth and Herbert S. Zim
Golden Press, 1967

Trees and Shrubs:

Manual of the Trees of North America (2 Vol.)
Charles S. Sargent
Dover Books

Trees of North America; A Guide to Field Identification
C. Frank Brockman
Golden Press, 1979

Natural History of Trees of Eastern and Central North America
Donald Curloss Peattie
Houghton-Mifflin Co., 1950

Natural History of Western Trees
Donald Curloss Peattie
Houghton-Mifflin Co., 1953

A Field Guide to Trees and Shrubs
(The Peterson Field Guide Series)
George A. Petrides
Houghton-Mifflin Co., 1972

Important Trees of Eastern Forests
Edited by R. W. Neelands
U.S. Department of Agriculture, 1974

Master Tree Finder
May Theilgaard Watts
Nature Study Guild, 1963

Winter Tree Finder
May Theilgaard Watts and Tom Watts
Nature Study Guild, 1970

Wildflowers and Weeds:

A Field Guide to Wildflowers of Northeastern and North-Central North America
Roger Tory Peterson and Margaret McKenny
Houghton-Mifflin Co., 1981

Wildflowers and Weeds
Booth Courtenay and James H. Zimmerman
Van Nostrand Reinhold Co., 1972

*Look At A Flower
Anne Ophelia T. Dowden
thomas Y. Crowell Co., 1972

Wild Green Things In the City: A Book of Weeds
Anne Ophelia T. Dowden
Thomas Y. Crowell Co., 1972

*Who Named the Daisy? Who Named the Rose?
Mary Durant
Congdon and Weed, 1976

Pods: Wildflowers and Weeds in Their
Final Beauty
Jane K. Embertson
Scribners, 1979

How to Identify Grasses and Grasslike
Plants
H. D. Harrington
Swallow Press, 1977

Illustrated Flora of the Northern United
States and Canada (3 Vol.)
Nathaniel Britton and Addison Brown
Dover Publications

Growing Wildflowers; A Gardner's
Guide
Marie Sperka
Harper and Row, 1973

Prairie Primer
Stan Nichols and Lynn Entine
University of Wisconsin Extension, 1978

The Prairie Garden; 70 Native Plants
You Can Grow in Town or Country
J. Robert Smith
University of Wisconsin Press, 1980

American Wildlife and Plants; A Guide
to Wildlife Food Habits
Alexander C. Martin, Herbert S. Zim, and
Arnold Nelson
Dover Books

Manual of Grasses of the United States (2
Vol.)
A. S. Hitchcock
Dover Books

Common Aquatic Weeds
L. W. Weldon and R. D. Blackburn
Dover Books

Leaves: Their Amazing Lives and
Strange Behavior
James Poling
Holt, Rinehart, and Winston, 1971

The Amazing Seeds
Ross E. Hutchins
Dodd, Mead, and Co., 1965

The Dictionary of Useful Plants
Nelson Coon
Rodale Press

*Plant and Planet
Anthony Huxley
Viking Press, 1974

A Field Guide to Wild Edible Plants of
Eastern and Central North America
(The Peterson Field Guide Series)
Lee K. Peterson
Houghton-Mifflin Co., 1977

How to Know the Grasses
Richard W. Pohl
Wm. C. Brown Co., 1978

*Face of North America; The Natural History of a Continent
Peter Farb
Harper and Row, 1964

Invertebrates:

A Field Guide to the Insects of America
North of Mexico
(The Peterson Field Guide Series)
Donald J. Borror and Richard E. White
Houghton-Mifflin Co., 1970

Butterflies and Moths
(A Golden Field Guide)
Robert T. Mitchell and Herbert S. Zim
Golden Press, 1977

A Field Guide to Butterflies
(The Peterson Field Guide Series)
Alexander B. Klots
Houghton-Mifflin Co.

Spiders and Their Kin
(A Golden Field Guide)
Herbert W. Levi
Golden Press, 1968

Ten Little Housemates
Karl von Frisch
Pergamon, 1960

Where They Go In Winter
Margaret Waring Buck
Abingdon Press, 1968

*Near Horizons
Edwin Way Teale
Dodd, Mead, and Co., 1942

*A Guide to Observing Insect Lives
Donald W. Stokes
Little, Brown, and Co., 1983

Fish, Reptiles, and Amphibians:

A Guide to Field Identification: Amphibians of North America
Hobart M. Smith
Golden Press, 1978

A Field Guide to Reptiles and Amphibians of Eastern and Central North America
(The Peterson Field Guide Series)
Roger B. Conant
Houghton-Mifflin Co.

Snakes, the Keeper and the Kept
Carl Kauffeld
Doubleday and Co., 1969

Foul and Loathsome Creatures
Harry Parsons
Supply and Services Canada, 1976

Birds:

*The Life of Birds
Joel Carl Welty
W.B. Saunders Co., 1975

*The Audubon Encyclopedia of North American Birds
Edited by John K. Terres
Alfred A. Knopf, 1982

*A Guide to the Behavior of Common Birds
Donald W. Stokes
Little, Brown, and Co., 1979

A Field Guide to Birds' Nests (Found East of Mississippi River)
(The Peterson Field Guide Series)
Hal H. Harrison
Houghton-Mifflin Co.

The Wonder of Birds
Edited by Robert M. Poole
National Geographic Society, 1983

A Guide to Field Identification; Birds of North America
Chandler S. Robbins, Bertel Bruun, and Herbert S. Zim
Golden Press, 1983

A Field Guide to the Birds East of the Rockies
(The Peterson Field Guide Series)
Roger Tory Peterson
Houghton-Mifflin Co., 1980

The Audubon Society Master Guide to Birding (3 Vol.)
Edited by John Farrand, Jr.
Alfred A. Knopf, 1983

Mammals:

A Field Guide to Animal Tracks
(The Peterson Field Guide Series)
Olaus J. Murie
Houghton-Mifflin Co., 1974

A Field Guide to the Mammals
(The Peterson Field Guide Series)
William H. Burt and Richard P. Grossenheider
Houghton-Mifflin Co., 1976

The World of the White-Tailed Deer
Leonard Lee Rue III
Lippincott, 1962

The World of the Red Fox
Leonard Lee Rue III
Lippincott, 1969

The World of the Gray Squirrel
Frederick S. Barlow and Monica Shorten
Lippincott, 1973

Note: There are many more titles in this Living World series by Lippincott, including books about birds of prey, reptiles and amphibians, and other common species.

General Reference:

The Amateur Naturalist's Handbook
Vinson T. Brown
Prentice Hall, 1980

Reading the Woods: Seeing More in Nature's Familiar Faces
Vinson T. Brown
Stackpole Books, 1969

*A Guide to Nature in Winter
Donald W. Stokes
Little, Brown, and Co., 1976

*The Cousteau Almanac: An Inventory of Life on Our Water Planet
Jacques Cousteau and the Staff of the Cousteau Society
Doubleday and Co., 1981

*The Marvels of Animal Behavior
Edited by Thomas B. Allen
National Geographic Society, 1972

Our Wildlife Legacy
Durward Allen
Funk and Wagnalls, 1974

*The Web of Life
John H. Storer
New American Library, 1972

Nature's Design: A Practical Guide to Natural Landscaping
Carol A. Smyser
Rodale Press, 1982

Design With Nature
Ian McHarg
Doubleday and Co., 1971

The Last Landscape
William H. Whyte
Doubleday and Co., 1968

In Suspect Terrain
John McPhee
Farrar, Straus, Giroux, 1983

The Closing Circle; Man, Nature, and Technology
Barry Commoner
Alfred A. Knopf, 1971

Good Reading and Writing:

*Reading the Landscape of America
May Theilgaard Watts
Macmillan, 1975

*The Immense Journey
Loren Eiseley
Random House, 1957

ALSO: The Star Thrower, The Invisible Pyramid and others

*A Sand County Almanac
Aldo Leopold
Westminster: Ballantine Books, 1970

*Pilgrim at Tinker Creek
Annie Dillard
Harper's Magazine Press, 1974

ALSO: Teaching a Stone to Talk and others

*The Singing Wilderness
Sigurd Olson
Alfred A. Knopf, 1979

ALSO: Reflections From the North Country and others

The Great Chain of Life
Joseph Wood Krutch
Houghton-Mifflin Co., 1957

ALSO: The Voice of the Desert and others

Life on a Little-Known Planet
Howard Ensign Evans
E.P. Dutton, 1968

*Beyond Your Doorstep
Hal Borland
Alfred A. Knopf, 1968

ALSO: Hill Country Harvest, When the Legends Die and others

From Laurel Hill to Siler's Bog; the Walking Adventures of a Naturalist
John K. Terres
Alfred A. Knopf, 1969

*The Lives of a Cell; Notes of a Biology Watcher
Lewis Thomas
Viking Press, 1974

ALSO: The Medusa and the Snail and others

The Year of the Whale
Victor B. Scheffer
Scribner's, 1969

The Sense of Wonder
Rachel Carson
Harper and Row, 1965

ALSO: Silent Spring

The Forest and the Sea; A Look at the
Economy of Nature and the Ecology of
Man
Marston Bates
Random House, 1960

*The John McPhee Reader
  Edited by William L. Howarth
  Farrar, Straus, and Giroux, 1976

*Where the Sky Began; Land of the Tall-
  grass Prairie
  John Madson
  Houghton-Mifflin Co., 1983

Spring In Washington
Louis J. Halle
Atheneum, 1963

A Season of Birds
Dion Henderson
Tamarack Press, 1976

*Wildlings
  Mary Leister
  Stemmer House Publishers, 1976

*Desert Solitaire: A Season In the Wilder-
  ness
  Edward L. Abbey
  McGraw-Hill, 1968

*North With the Spring, 1951
  Journey Into Summer, 1960
  Autumn Across America, 1956
  Wandering Through Winter, 1965
  (The American Seasons Series)
  Edwin Way Teale
  Dodd, Mead, and Co.

  ALSO: A Naturalist Buys an Old Farm
  and others

*The Klamath Knot: Explorations of Myth
  and Evolution
  David Rains Wallace
  Sierra Club, 1983

*Hen's Teeth and Horses' Toes
  Stephen Jay Gould
  Norton, 1983

  ALSO: The Panda's Thumb and others

The Blue Planet
Louise B. Young
Little, Brown, and Co., 1983

The Primal Place
Robert Finch
Norton, 1983

Of Wolves of Men
Barry Holstun Lopez
Charles Scribner's, 1978

Writing Sampler Credits

Permission to reprint excerpts from the following books has been granted by the publishers.

Chapter One
>Wildlings</u>
Mary Leister
Stemmer House Publishers, 1976
2627 Caves Road
Owings Mills, Maryland 21117

Chapter Two
<u>Reading the Landscape of America</u>
May Theilgaard Watts
Macmillan Publishing Company, 1957
866 Third Avenue
New York, New York 10022

Chapter Three
<u>Desert Solitaire</u>
Edward Abbey
Don Congdon Associates, Inc., 1968
111 Fifth Avenue
New York, New York 10003

Chapter Four
<u>Wilderness, the Discovery of a Continent of Wonder</u>
Rutherford H. Platt
Dodd, Mead and Company, Inc., 1961
71 Fifth Avenue
New York, New York 10003